Learn Your Story, Find Your Power

Using Emotional Awareness to Enrich Your Self and Your Relationships

Learn Your Story, Find Your Power

Using Emotional Awareness
to Enrich Your Self
and Your Relationships

Nancy Floyd Harshman, Ph.D.

 ABBEY PRESS

Cover art: The tapestry depicted on the cover was designed and created by Linda P. Schapper for the 1991 Week of Prayer for Christian Unity. The original tapestry (which measures six-and-a-half feet square) was commissioned by Graymoor Ecumenical Institute, Graymoor, New York, where it is now displayed.

Cover design: Scott Wannemuehler

Library of Congress Catalog Number
92-73172

ISBN 0-87029-248-X

Published by Abbey Press
St. Meinrad Archabbey
St. Meinrad, IN 47577

Dedication

To my family —
Bo, Andy, Erin, Casey, & Charlie

In celebration of our
joy and pain
and the privilege of
sharing life with you!

Contents

Acknowledgements:

One evening my eighty-six-year-old grandmother, her aged eyes wide with intelligence and spirit, dictated to me the history of the Hunter Clan, which she had chronicled years before. She spoke the names with deep respect born of her knowledge of each person's contribution to the family. It was an amazing evening for the ten-year-old I was: receiving the attention and love of this very special woman while being inducted into the role of family archivist. It was also my initiation into systemic thinking. That evening is alive in me still. Thank you, Margaret Hunter Lytle Floyd, for that evening's ritual, the reverence for family, and the role you bestowed on me.

To my parents, Robert Lytle Floyd (1904–1988) and Jean Rettew Floyd (1910–1972), and my siblings, Barbara Floyd McGowan, Lynne Floyd Sexton, Robert John Floyd, and James Rettew Floyd: I am deeply grateful for the fire and forces of our family reservoir and all the challenge and blessing that it offers.

Karen Katafiasz, my editor, was able to bring our right and left brains together in the editing process. It was an enlightening, dialectic process in which we prodded and polished the work to completion.

Mike and Joanne Tressler, dear friends whose family's path has crossed and paralleled ours for years, were generous in the time they took to give me professional and personal feedback.

Susan Vetter and Carolyn Draheim are my "agents"; they are also my secretaries. They are powerful agents in many senses of the word: promoters, technical assistants, interpreters, investigators, to name a few.

Paul Edward Harshman, Jr., has been my partner in the most important adventures of my life. In this one, in addition to cooking and cleaning, he cut, pasted, and one-finger typed endless drafts (no computer!). He was willing to delve into the structure of the writing, risking more opportunities to collide with me. He was unfailing and bold in his partnering and loving.

Introduction

"And he will raise you up…" As we were walking out of the church, the song "On Eagle's Wings" resounded from behind, around, and within. "And he will raise you up…," the refrain repeated as his grandsons lifted my father's casket from the church steps.

There was some mysterious resolution and promise in that hymn. The cycle of life was glimpsed and comprehended for a brief moment. The generational wheel was turning. There was a sense of my father, his physical presence lost to us but his spirit not lost. Here were these young men bearing the body of one they love and came from—a special burden falling on their shoulders: to bear death, which they are just learning to touch and which is foreign in their strong, young manhood. And we, these children of his, are now more knowledgeable about dying, but still ignorant compared to our father.

A memory came back to me: my father walking alone in the backyard at night after he was notified of his mother's death. As a 14-year-old, I observed that walk and sensed his pain and the too-largeness of the experience he was having. It was amazing to see. I felt shaken to see that something could be too much for my dad, and at the same time I felt immense tenderness and care for him.

It's good that life repeats the cycle again and again. Each time our place in the cycle advances, and we gain a new perspective. Comprehension inches ahead.

The vision of my sons and their cousins lifting my father's body is a powerful metaphor to me. It witnesses the generational flow of life and the way learning about living is transmitted. It is a vision of the mystical, spiritual legacy of the family of our origin. It is real. Every family has this legacy: the myths, the traditions, the dysfunctions, and the triumphs. It's rich material to study, worth the investment of time and energy. It's our own story.

We are moved by, we resonate with, the stories of other persons in films, books, theater, and concerts. The resonance comes from some particular feature of our story. The stories of others that we hold most dear are those that embody some part of our own story. Their meaning derives from their relevance to ourselves. We are learning about living and about ourselves in the stories of others. We read, watch, or listen to the story. In memory, it is the subject of our reverie. Its music may surround us. The experience of replaying the story, in whatever form, strengthens our connection to the learning that the story imparts, the value or truth of life it expresses. Yet, strangely, in the midst of these powerful renditions of the stories of others, we resist replaying our own.

There is promise— "And he will raise you up..." The words offer the promise that my father's existence is not contained by that box. As I learn about my own story, there is more promise. I can raise up beyond my previous level of knowledge and functioning. And I am not contained in the past.

In our families, we are introduced to experiences involving intimacy, belonging, and accomplishment. Just as language is learned by an infant through an infinite number of repetitions, so the emotional life of the family repeats experiences that are stored in emotional memory. Millions of interactions repeat and get stored before we are verbal, countless others during early verbal development. A great deal of what we "know" does not get verbalized and entered into rational memory. But the information is available if we seek it.

I have seen the phenomenon operate when, as a therapist, I ask a client a question about something that she does not know she knows. The question loosens something and up comes a bit of information. The information gets verbalized and then can be encoded into conscious memory. It becomes transformed into information that she knows she knows. Now the information can be employed to make a decision or a choice, to be expressed, or to operate consciously as a value.

When a person experiences emotion, emotional memory becomes considerably more available. Emotion allows access to "holograms" of some of those early exposures to intimacy, admonitions, expression—or lack of expression—of feelings, and meanings made about various situations. Asking a question like "When have I felt like this before?" produces the emotional memory, or at least a trace of it. It's much like sitting at a computer and requesting information that was previously programmed in.

The computer makes decisions, handles data, and functions according to the programming it has received. The experience in our families is the programming we received, and it operates consciously or unconsciously. When a computer malfunctions, the programmer of the software is often consulted. If we know what the programmer knows—how the program was written— we have power with the computer.

In the same way, if we find out how the program was written in our family, we have immense power with ourselves. We can reprogram: change beliefs and meanings, express what was stifled, teach material that was inadvertently left out, heal trauma, and take opportunities previously missed. The power and control we can have continue to increase as we live. Our knowledge, our consciousness imparts the power.

This book is about elucidating the purpose and the joy of learning your own story. It's not about condemning anyone and certainly not about blaming anyone. It's about picking up your own power and being open to the cycles and the generational flow that teaches and empowers. Your own story will "raise you up."

Chapter one

Family of Origin Experience: Finding Power in Learning Your Story

I have great reverence for families. They are sacred units. We live in a time that stretches the traditional concept of family. There are a variety of ways persons form families today and a variety of configurations in which they live. However formed, each family has its own spirituality, the life force that is the combination of all the lives that have formed the circle. And each family has its own emotional expression of that spirituality. Our early experience with the spirit of our family writes the program for our later functioning. The program is not irrevocably written, but it is powerfully written. All the persons in a family have made their mark on the family's spirit. The generational accumulation of the contributions of all those who went before has life, long after death has claimed their bodies. The generational accumulation passes on culture, values, traditions, and rituals. Who we are in the world and how we function in it are

7

shaped by our experience in our families.

A genealogical search and the family tree that results from it can generate interest and excitement. But the names on the tree are just the symbols that mark the logistical position of the persons in the family. In terms of the power of the family, there is much more to be excited about. Who were the persons and what were their beliefs? How did their spirits shape the family they were in and, generations later, contribute to the one we are in? What had life taught them, how did they pass it on, how have we received their contributions? And what are we passing on?

There is even more that happens in families than the downward transmission of the generational accumulation. Each person in every family offers numerous opportunities for the family spirit to be changed and expanded. These opportunities occur when there is a collision between the downward generational flow of the family and the growth and development of any of its members. Families can be changed from the bottom up. In the process of their own becoming, our young demand that we stretch and learn from their experience and perspective. For instance, when a family particular about protocol gets a child born to it whose life rhythm is more free-flowing and less formal, there is a collision. The family has a chance to evaluate its adherence to decorum and consider loosening a little. Families are challenged to learn and grow while their young members are developing. Our young continue to make those demands of the generational accumulation over the course of their life span, even while the next generation challenges them.

Those people we are born to and grow up with, as well as the ones we birth and raise, are more powerful for us than any other people on earth. The power comes from the relatedness formed by birth, vow, and adoption and from the spirituality that grows from that relatedness. The family is the enchanted circle. We have to return to our family to do the work necessary to transcend it. The family holds the original energy, the dynamism from which we came. We were formed there and must return there to re-form and move ahead. When life delivers a message and a new learning is formed, it is in the family that the fresh clay, the greenware, is fired. The family is the kiln. Going back to the family and, in their presence, being able to hold onto some newly formed behavior or skill are essential to its permanence.

Emotion as access to your story

Families are not all good or all bad. Each family leaves a rich and varied legacy, regardless of its particular degree of functionality. Our experience in the family of our origin leaves its mark deep within the tissue of our bodies. Emotion is the expression of that experience. Situations of our present life echo feelings stored in the emotional memory tissue. The flood of feelings that thunders forth contains all the emotional data necessary for resolution of past as well as present dilemmas. Human beings are able, therefore, to become incredibly powerful and generative. The drama of each person's family story holds the emotional details that can release the power. It is the power of the human spirit; it is trustworthy.

Being alive involves both body and soul and learning how to infuse each with the other so that body holds and nurtures spirit and spirit animates body. Being alive is about allowing connection and communication between body and soul. Being alive is about allowing body and soul to meet and merge; at that juncture and in that act is the experience of human spirituality. The emotional memory tissues are the places of communication and connection deep inside the human body where the sensory data, the experiences of the body, meet the spirit. The information that is exchanged there and even the tissue in which the exchange takes place can be perceived through feelings. I believe that, while we are alive, human spirituality is that corporal. The emotions are the expression

> *Childhood was where a million learnings were made, where beliefs about ourselves and the world around us initiated, where our goals, values, and ways of presenting ourselves were formed.*

of the meeting of body and soul. Aliveness is the result of the meeting of body and soul. Aliveness is an emotional experience; it is spiritual, and therefore it is limitless. Aliveness does not need to diminish with age. Perhaps aliveness may increase so greatly with age that it becomes too much for the body to contain. What if that's what death is: the body expires when the aliveness becomes too much for it? Aging, then, is about coming more alive. Aging offers the chance to learn how to use body and soul together to expand the capacity to enjoy life and to understand its significance and its sequel.

Human spirituality develops out of experience within the body. Personhood develops out of experience in the family. Emotion is the expression of both experiences, as well as the access to both.

Therapy: taking the puzzle pieces out of the box

Therapy is like the sidelines of a ball game. It is a place to get out of the action, reflect about what's going on, and plan a new strategy. Therapy is also like life. Both are opportunities that present and resurrect all the emotional data we need for resolution, decision, healing, and expansion. Therapy is like life also in that it takes place in the context of relationship. The therapist, however, is not in the client's life. The therapist is on the sidelines, but not as a coach. Coaches have an investment in the outcome. Therapists need to be emotionally available and safe persons to be with. If they are invested in the outcome, they are no longer safe.

In therapy you get to be just who you are. You get to say what you feel, and you get to explore what situations and messages attended your arrival on this earth. You get to meet yourself and see what you want to do about it. Many of us got the message that it was not OK to talk about what we experienced—not even to ourselves. Not being able to talk out loud about what is happening is like trying to solve a 500-piece puzzle without taking it out of the box. In therapy, the pieces get to come out of the box. When we see how the puzzle pieces fit, we can begin to make cognitive and emotional sense of the facts of our life. Gradually the mechanisms of our programming and functioning become accessible and employable. Then the unconscious begins to push or drag less. Instead, the unconscious begins to subsidize personal power and spirit.

The unconscious becomes a resource for us to return to and wander around in, feeling the details of the personal story on file there. Again, emotion is the key. Emotions invigorate, animate, and exhilarate. Emotions transform the dates and details of a personal history into a living drama.

My office is a "living room." Persons enter and the stories of their lives unfold. It is their stress, pain, and crisis that bring them. They are not crazy, although their pain can create that illusion for both themselves and others. It is an insult to persons in pain to believe that it is their ignorance that perpetuates the pain. At first look, one may wonder why she doesn't move away from the abuse, or why he continues self-defeating behavior. But, no, persons who come for therapy are not ignorant or crazy. As their stories unfold, the pain makes perfect sense, and all the wisdom of each person is called upon in the effort to respond and grow. It is arrogant to try to modify another person's behavior. I do, all too frequently, wander into that territory. It is my fear and some details of my own story that activate my arrogance. I do believe that each person who enters my "living room" is powerful and competent. Each person is fully capable of leaning into the ordeal life has delivered and learning what it has come to teach.

Crisis: an opportunity to learn your story

Pain, stress, and crisis crack persons open. Much of the psychological and emotional order of life gets blown apart. Whatever was buried or neatly packed away gets exhumed. I picture a yard with grass growing green and even. Suddenly the yard is full of craters, blown-up chunks of stuff unearthed. A marital crisis, a stillborn infant, a job lost, a child reaching adolescence, a disease, a death—these are the bombs. If we could connect the craters like a dot-to-dot puzzle, we would see the outline of a personal story. It is the crisis, stress, and pain that present the "opportunity" to explore this story.

It doesn't feel like an opportunity. The full, green grass felt soothing, pleasant, and settled. The craters can certainly be replaced and the yard made green again. It takes a lot of work and often is frustrating because this is likely not the first replanting. But eventually the stuff won't be stuffed back into the earth. And this is truly the moment of crisis, when the old ways don't produce the same results. That's when facing the "opportunity" becomes the only alternative. That's when persons feel crazy and when they are likely to come to a "living room."

One morning I overheard some young men talking at breakfast. They had been out all night and were determined to carry the night's activities into the day. They were spirited and very carefree. As they settled into breakfast, one young man said, "My mom carries the weight of the world on her shoulders; she worries about everybody." I don't know the young man or his mother. But I do know that she doesn't carry the weight of the world incidentally or accidentally. There are good reasons why his mother does that. And, I wonder, what has encouraged this young man to be so carefree?

Good reasons—"good" in the sense of solid and understandable. We need to understand the reasons. Perhaps this young man has seen what the weight of the world does to shoulders, and he may be determined in his carefreeness to avoid that. I believe it is this kind of understanding that allow options and choices. This young reveler needs to be able to choose when to be carefree and when to face responsibility. If he just runs from the weight of the world, he may run into trouble. Moments of intense pain, stress, and crisis create the opportunity to learn the story so we can understand the reasons and have the options.

I have the privilege of sitting down time and again and having my ears and the space of my room entrusted with persons' pain. I listen as the stories unfold, and the best thing I can do is to make sure they take more and more of their story with them when they leave. We look for what today's pain resonates with from the past, following clues in feelings, language, and situations. It is awesome to watch the process. Their stories are about the roots of their origin and the relationships that surrounded them. That early experience resides within them, and so their mother and father and all their life experience reside inside. All the ideas, values, rules, traditions—the cultures of the families that joined to produce them—reside within them.

I see persons begin to realize what a fascinating story they have, that it is a drama, poignant and important. I watch persons lay claim to their past and their emotional selves. In doing so, they become powerful in the present. A great deal that made no sense begins to make incredible sense. In this process, the pain forges the power.

Carol's story: "It's about me."
Carol is 38 years old. She and her husband Kevin have three

children. They have been involved at church, and both contribute their talents to the kids' activities. They have a nice social life and enjoy their friends. Each has separate interests that are rewarding and provide many social contacts for the couple. For the past six months, Kevin has been behaving differently. At first, Carol hardly gave it a thought when he stayed longer at work and made commitments that took more time from the family. But when Kevin became increasingly irritable and silent, the first alarm went off inside Carol. It wasn't a loud alarm, but it aroused many of her systems. More alert, she noticed when the irritability occurred, what had preceded it, and what had followed. Only a few weeks passed before she was quite sure about which behaviors of hers or the kids triggered Kevin's surliness. Carol was careful now about when to ask for help with household chores. She tried to make things nicer for Kevin when he came home and to have the kids more settled down so he could relax. All of this made very little difference in Kevin's anger and silence. The few times that seemed to improve the situation reinforced Carol's determination to continue her efforts.

After several weeks, Kevin's behavior took on new dimensions. He began drinking more on social occasions, often resulting in embarrassment to Carol. People began to look at her sympathetically, especially when Kevin was sarcastic or indifferent toward her. The second alarm had gone off inside her, and now not only was she cognitively alert but her adrenal system was working overtime as well.

Carol's appetite decreased. She felt a little nauseated most of the time. She could feel her heart beating faster when she tried to figure things out. At times, she was feeling shaky and couldn't think as clearly as she was used to or needed to. Thoughts became more circular as she tried to discover what was wrong. And the circle was closing in. "It's me! He doesn't like what I do. He doesn't want to be with me."

When she was asked, "When have you felt like this before?" Carol's inside emotional parts began to search for the answer before her brain fully comprehended the question. Carol realized she had felt this way as a child when her dad had lost his temper. He was a good and loving man who worked hard to support eight children. At times her dad's stress would climax in a rage. She had been able to sense the tension building and would try to get her sisters and brothers to quiet down. She would help with dinner, clean the house, and answer the phone on the first ring. As she put effort into controlling her dad's temper, the more likely she was to be in the middle of things when his temper would go. The anger that exploded created a belief inside the child that Carol was: "It's me! Dad doesn't like what I do." It was a relief to feel now about those times and memories long since buried and to express some of what she had never been able to get out before. Carol began to recognize that there were other times she picked up on and tried to manage the tension of others—as a child with her teachers in the classroom and currently with her director of nursing at the hospital.

It is fairly easy to see that Carol did not cause her dad's rage. It was the stress of his life and his own psychic mechanisms that turned his stress into rage. In other words, it was not about Carol. Maybe Kevin's behavior is not about her either. This awareness does not solve the problem between Carol and Kevin, but Carol's reaction to Kevin's behavior can be different. She can discharge the emotion that is the residue of previous situations, and she can entertain the idea that she is not the cause of Kevin's behavior. Realizing that "it's not about me" can reduce her anxiety and confusion. Relieved of the responsibility of causing the problem, Carol can begin to help herself in this distressing situation. She also has the opportunity to realize that her husband must be struggling with something very difficult.

Carol reacted to the family pattern of becoming volcanic with feelings by becoming first an alert observer and then a creative problem-solver. She developed excellent skills early in her life, and there were many occasions to use the skills. She was quick to pick up subtleties in school subjects. Her competence in organizing, managing, and problem-solving made her very successful at the hospital and capable of combining a career with motherhood.

The shift in Carol's marriage released feelings deep within

her, some of which resonate from this earlier time. One of the craters that resulted from the explosion in her life contains the memories and feelings of Carol the child. Another crater contains a belief carried out of that early time: "It's about me!" As we walk in Carol's exploded yard, we can see the outline of some of her story. The willingness of a child to try to make a difficult situation better, and her persistence in that effort, developed skills in her that were used throughout childhood with her teachers and friends. As an adult, she has become a powerful and willing woman, who can attend to and manage a great many things. Unfortunately, the child that she was formed a belief that her value as a person depends on whether she is successful at managing everything she is willing to try.

Power and powerlessness

Our early experience in our family conveys the most powerful, nonverbal teachings. The learning is communicated experientially, and it is stored unconsciously. All of our senses are involved; therefore, the experiences are rich, colorful, and emotional. Experiences like learning to ride a bike, losing a beloved pet, being scolded or praised are memories rich in detail and feeling. Our early experiences in the family of our origin shape, direct, and lay the deepest meaning on our lives for all the years to come. It is our emotions that provide access to this unconscious storehouse of experience. This means that we are not powerless with the unfolding of our lives.

The concept of powerlessness has generated confusion and controversy about its meaning and application. I find the idea of powerlessness helpful, not to claim an internal lack of strength or capacity, but to indicate those things which it is useless to try to be powerful with. It is useless to use my strength or capacity to try to make the sun come up, make a chicken skate, or iron the ocean. Trying to iron the ocean would take great courage and effort, but would result in exhaustion and feelings of failure and inadequacy. It is important to know that I am powerless with the ocean.

It is useless to try to stop the effects of caffeine, alcohol, sugar, a laxative, or poison once any of these substances has entered my bloodstream. I can ingest an antidote, but humans lack the capacity to nullify the effect of a substance in the bloodstream. It is also useless to try to make someone, other than myself, study, listen, see, or stop. I cannot make a person with an eating disorder eat, or stop eating. I cannot cause an alcoholic to drink, or make the alcoholic stop drinking.

I can tell you my ideas and tell you what I am concerned about. I can say what I feel and ask you to stop. But I am powerless to make you do anything. Acknowledging that I am powerless with you keeps me in my yard, on my side of the fence, and that is where I can be powerful. This demarcation of who I am powerful with, and who I am not, marks the boundary between you and me. Acknowledging this boundary is essential to my integrity and to yours.

The experience of powerlessness increases as we try to control anything over which we have no power. The scene from the film *Song of the South* when Br'er Rabbit decides to make Tar Baby talk is a wonderful example of what happens when we try to exert force where we have no power. Br'er Rabbit was very happy and carefree as he hopped along and sang "Good mornin' " to all the creatures around him. As each creature responded, the rabbit's delight increased. So did his sense of power, unfortunately. When Tar Baby did not return his greeting, Br'er Rabbit decided to make Tar Baby talk. He tried, politely, then firmly. Then he commanded Tar Baby to talk. He would not be stopped or slighted like this, so Br'er Rabbit decided to smack a "good mornin' " out of Tar Baby. The rabbit ended up stuck all over Tar Baby. Personal power is protected and preserved by a thorough sense of what one is powerful with and what one is not powerful with.

"It didn't affect me": denial as powerlessness

There is a way to become powerless, to lose internal strength and capacity, and not even know it. That way is through denial. Denial produces just such results. With the rich legacy of family of origin experience, denial sounds like: "That is in the past," or "It didn't affect me," or "I had a happy childhood," (as if "happy" means there is no story to tell). A childhood is not so black or white as this. Even in a devastating, abuse-filled childhood there was some respite, some kindness, some play. But the issue is not whether childhood was good or bad. Childhood was where a million learnings were made, where beliefs about ourselves and the world around us initiated, where our significant relationships were established, and therefore, where our knowledge-base about relationships was formed. Our goals, values, and ways of presenting ourselves to the world were formed there in childhood. Maintaining a position that the past has no effect, or that childhood was happy so don't bother with it, is ignorant. Denial of the breadth and depth of childhood's significance has tremendous impact. Denial cuts off access to almost every means by which we developed our internal strength and capacities. Wiped out in a single stroke is the value of all the meanings, beliefs, emotional resonance, culture, and traditions that the child you were experienced and stored. As powerful an impact would be to erase from yourself all the knowledge and nuances you gathered about language as a child. Gone. No effect.

What is this denial about? Why do we do this? Is it a feeling of trespassing? It would be our own experience we are trespassing in. Is it a betrayal of parents? That's a big issue. As children, we needed them. Whether they were wonderful or horrible by our child's perception, or alternately both, we needed them. And we needed at least one to be a good parent. Getting curious about and fascinated by what was learned in childhood is not for the purpose of blaming or betraying parents. In fact, getting curious creates the opportunity to get to know who they were.

Knowing parents as persons, not icons

I have been taught and I have learned that part of growing up is coming to know one's parents as the persons they were, not as the icons of a child's perception. Getting to know them as persons means realizing that they were neither wonderful nor horrible, but that they were as human as we are, foibles and faults right next to assets and strengths. Getting to know them as persons is what to do with parents after we don't need them to tell us to button our coats or to save our money. Meeting our parents as persons is an important part of growing up. Some of us live to be older than our parents got to be. It is important to experience ourselves as peers of our parents even though parents will always be 'bigger' than we are since we are their children. There is a wonderful scene from the film *Field of Dreams* where Ray Kinsella encounters his father as a young man about his own age. The meeting of father and son, the visual encounter, is powerful. They take the field and play ball. For a brief moment, father and son meet each other on the same plane while time stands still. Powerful experience. Essential moments to allow. We do get to stand where our parents have stood.

The most sense I can make out of the denial of our family of origin legacy is that early on it became a goal to not be affected by Mom's temper or Dad's drinking or to bury and forget whatever it was that happened last night. This was survival, defense, coping. Even in families where experiences were more subtle than drinking or raging, lessons were covertly taught about not feeling and not talking. There is no reason to remember if you can't look back to talk and feel about an experience in order to understand it. So denial of early experience is an expression of loyalty to family mores and rules, and it is a remnant of childhood coping skills and defenses.

Many of us learned that it was not acceptable to talk about what we felt or saw, just as it was not acceptable to burp at the table. Many learned it was not all right to ask questions about certain parts of our bodies or certain aspects of life: sex, death, fighting. Just don't do it! It was not all right for many of us to question adults when we saw inconsistencies or sensed dishonesty or a cover-up. Pretend you don't see it. We adjusted our behavior and learned to cope according to the particular code of the family we grew up in.

Respecting, not colluding with, childhood coping skills

I believe that the coping skills of a child—the child that you and I were—need to be very much respected, but not colluded with. Colluding would mean making an agreement with ourselves not to ask ourselves to change or enlarge the coping skills and defenses we learned as children. Underneath that line of defense is all of the child's emotional programming, the entire data base. It is the mission control center. The success of the flight depends on the knowledge and wisdom of mission control personnel. As adults, we can get behind the line of defense and get into the data base by remembering and feeling about our memories. There are amazing experiences to be had in the process.

Each child has her own unique reaction to any particular family pattern, and out of that reaction and repeated experience with the family pattern develop the coping skills and needs of the adult. My family of origin worried a lot. My mom was the second grand worrier; her mother was the grandest worrier. I don't want to demean my mother and grandmother; there had been reasons to generate the anxiety. My maternal grandparents must have been extremely wealthy in their early married years. It has been told to me that my grandfather would give my uncle $50 to take to a record store in the early 1920s to spend on a Saturday afternoon. My uncle, an extremely bright person, had meningitis as a toddler and had totally lost his vision. The 1929 stock market crash devastated the family financially. My once wealthy grandfather became a traveling book salesman, and his wife and children moved every two to three months to stay ahead of the bill collectors. My grandmother had also told me many stories of the disease and accidents that brought death to six of her thirteen siblings. It is very understandable why my grandmother looked ahead and predicted in a pessimistic fashion. On visits, or as a small child at my mom's side while she talked with her mother on the phone, I heard one or both sides of the worrying. I wanted my grandmother to be happier and my mom to be less upset when she got off the phone. There is a little Nancy who set about problem-solving and dreaming up ways to make her mom and grandmother happier. Big job, little girl. There is an adult Nancy who can be activated into those same pursuits. The switch is quite often thrown without my knowledge, and I can be days or weeks into the pursuit without conscious consent. Yes, even years into it.

The family pattern was worrying; my roles were problem-solving and happiness-generation. These roles created a varied and lengthy list of skills that have been useful. The employment of those skills has also sometimes been my undoing. I need to know when the switch is likely to be thrown, so I can consciously participate in deciding whether it's my problem to solve or if anyone wants more happiness and if it's my place to generate it.

Ed's story: personal value from being the rescuer

Ed is a human resources manager for a substantial local

company. He is a solid businessman with a sincere interest in what is happening around him. He has a high profile in his community because of the time he commits to a variety of volunteer activities. Ed is a Little League coach and a Big Brother. He has been at the helm of a variety of events involving local business support for schools, as well as projects with the inner city and the elderly. Ed is the kind of man whose assertiveness and strength create a macho veneer, but it is transparent. Visible beneath are the warmth and compassion that prompt him to be available to the concerns of his community. Though his profile is high, his style is low-key and gentle. He is personal, ready with a joke or some chatter to lift a spirit.

His kids, three teenage boys, are proud of him, and their friends enjoy being around him. Sara works hard to support the activities of her husband and sons, keeps the house, and excels in her position as a paralegal assistant. It would seem as if the only thing lacking in this busy family is enough time.

The boys used to wait patiently for more time with their dad. Now, as teenagers, their own interests take them away from the house more and they don't notice missing Dad so much. Sara still longs for more time with Ed. She is drawn to his warmth and gentleness, though it barely brushes over her before he is involved away again.

This man who has so much is in a state of shock because last weekend Sara discovered Ed's emotional involvement with a young woman he was mentoring at the office. His shock comes from the crisp edge of reality brought on by his wife's discovery. Sara's devastation and anguish turn the lights on for Ed, and he is seeing some of his behavior clearly for the first time. It has been delusional, like a puppy love, full of secret meetings and notes, a little touching, a lot of pretending. The young woman was so vulnerable, so needing. He was the hero, the rescuer. To his sons, he's not the hero now. And Ed is literally undone; he cannot understand how or why he let this happen.

All that was intact and in good working order in this family's life is scattered and exposed now. He feels terrible, but it is a chance for Ed to find some answers to his whys and take responsibility for himself. He can hardly stand the uncertainty that is within and around him now.

This uncertainty has a familiar resonance, like an uncertainty experienced years ago, and he could hardly stand it then. The uncertainty existed in the gap between Ed's dad and mom. It was very subtle, with not much going on that one could see or put a finger on, but the feeling was strong. His dad worked hard and depended on Ed to cover some jobs at home. His mom had her hands full with five kids, and Ed, as the oldest son, was the role model for the other kids. Ed became the glue between this busy mom and dad. He served as Dad's liaison at home, doing some of the jobs a dad would do. He became Mom's hero, behaving in ways she was very proud of. He learned to become sensitive to his mom's needs and feelings, and he brought his warmth and compassion to those needs. The untouchable, almost imperceptible uncertainty lay in the fact that Mom and Dad were not connected. Their busyness consumed their energy and sometimes made them crabby with each other and the kids. No wellspring of intimacy had developed between them to be a resource and restoration to the couple. Ed had become the resource. He was like the boy with his hand in the dike, having hardly a clue as to what kind of hole he was plugging and having no idea how to talk about it or ask for help.

As I learn my story, I see how I act out of it. Then I can choose what to keep of the rich legacy, what to relinquish, what to change.

Ed became skilled in ways the world appreciates in a man. He was very handy and clever. He was resourceful and had many creative ideas. He knew how to take charge, be strong, and say no. He also knew how to discern when a person had a feeling. He had provided many solutions to a needing woman before he became entangled outside his marriage. He had been entangled inside his parent's marriage.

His roles were to please Dad and to protect and connect with Mom, as well as to be the leader of the family. The family pattern was lack of intimacy between Mom and Dad. Ed developed the need to be prized and valued for his accomplishments. His coping skills of rescuing, being the hero, and being the problem-solver brought him much recognition and satisfaction. Those roles and coping skills left him vulnerable, however. He was always busy away from himself—so busy that he had little conscious time to know about his own needs and feelings. And that was the Achilles' heel of this fine man.

Ed had long been in the practice of knowing what those around him needed. Giving others what they needed became how he answered his own need to be valued. A strong connection got made between responding to others' needs and Ed's sense of value for himself as a person—so strong that he violated his own value system to maintain a sense of personal value. Sound like a contradiction? It is. When that contradiction exists within one's person, it is like being contorted. Or it is *a* being contorted. It is amazing to me how we get ourselves into just exactly the predicament that will highlight the contortion. And then we can see just how to untwist.

Getting curious—getting power

Denial can sabotage the opportunity, however. The contortion may be highlighted by the predicament, but if we cannot look because of some unspoken rule about family loyalty or an impossible promise to not be affected by the past, the opportunity is lost. The next predicament is usually larger, casting a greater highlight. If we stick with denial, the denial must grow larger with each larger predicament. Each of us has many opportunities to see the consequences of our behavior, and each time that we are able to explain a consequence away, the next consequence is destined to be bigger.

A young man may witness the devastation of his dad's drinking on the family. He determines that his life will not be affected by his father's behavior. He begins to make himself powerful in the ways his dad was not. He is already affected by Dad. His determination will develop wonderful skills and assets. But if he never stops to see that he is affected by his past, his assets can become liabilities. If Dad did not provide for the family, this young man's goal may be to provide. If he doesn't stop to be fascinated by how powerful he got in response to his dad's failure, the powerfulness can become drivenness.

If he can get curious and fascinated by the skills and coping mechanisms that developed from his experience with his father's behavior, he can be in charge of those skills. He can decide when to work and when to stop. If not, he will be driven by his experience with his father's behavior. His dad was driven by alcohol. Not only do the two men begin to become more alike in their behavior, but the effect on their families is the same. This second-generation man is gone working; his dad was gone drinking. Alcohol allowed his dad to rage at the family; his overwork fires him into rages. Work becomes more important and gets more time than the people he loves, just like Dad's alcohol became more important and got more time. Tragic. A good young man who made an important commitment loses control and begins to behave exactly the way he vowed not to.

There is a generational process going on. It is a powerful process. It can empower or it can devastate. Our choice. Denial invites devastation. Acknowledgement opens the door to freedom and allows the rich and varied legacy of the family of one's origin to be an open book, open for reference and resource.

A sense of our personal history is necessary to understand ourselves in any particular situation. Personal history reveals the "good reasons" underneath behavior and feelings. The reasons why: the young reveler has such a strong urge to be carefree; Carol tries so hard to keep people from feeling tense; Ed could become involved outside his marriage; a man may become so driven to provide. The good reasons are not excuses. Understanding the reasons allows one to have options and make choices instead of being driven by dynamics one has no knowledge of. Learning about the dynamics and reasons is not for the purpose of blaming. Blaming paralyzes. As I learn my story, I can begin to see how I act out of it. Then I can choose what to keep of the rich legacy, what to relinquish, what to change, and how to change it. Learning about your story is for the purpose of becoming powerful with yourself.

Chapter two

The Relationship Interplay: Using Dialectic Process, Observing "As If" Trances

A beautiful image remains for me that I once saw on a giant movie screen. The presentation was entitled *To Fly*. On the screen, purported to be three football fields in dimension, a series of scenes unfolded. The screen lit up first with huge profiles of a man and a woman in silhouette and a glimpse of water and sun behind them. There was a sense of intimacy and seclusion created. As the camera receded, more of the surroundings appeared on the screen. Now visible were several other persons as well, and a beach with a slice of the ocean's waves coming to shore. The image of the original couple was still strong. The impression was of two lovers sharing a beautiful part of nature with a few other people—a sense of individuals against the background of the power of the ocean. But the camera continued to gradually pull back and, in doing so, destroyed the previous image. This was a crowded beach, perhaps the Atlantic City

Boardwalk. The camera angle was large enough now to see hundreds of people, a little beach, and lots of bustling. The original image that was so touching remained in memory and sense even though, visually, it was obliterated. As the camera continued to recede, it revealed views of the city that held the beach, then the countryside around the city. The receding gathered speed, pulling the viewer back to outer space for a magnificent view of the earth. Still lingering were all the images between the first and this last stunning one. *To Fly* vividly portrayed the phenomenal experiences that humans are privy to, as we have learned to master this majestic means of transporation.

The immense and beautiful experience that unfolded on the screen is for me a powerful reminder of how much is going on in each moment, in any scene—much more than can possibly be comprehended in a single viewing. This vision reminds me that each encounter deserves to be approached with care and respect, for there is so much going on that will be beyond my awareness. I am very grateful for this perspective. It helps to keep the arrogance in check that would have me believe it is possible to fully size up a situation, to know all that is going on. How many angles and perspectives are necessary to understand any interaction? What are the stories embedded in the context of each situation, much like the silhouette of the original man and woman embedded in the view of the planet earth? It takes time and often a lot of work to determine at least some of what is going on.

It is not efficient in the short term to wonder about, reflect on, and inspect the different angles and origins of interactions. But often there is no other way to make a situation intelligible without some of this effort—unless we are willing to say that someone is wrong, or stupid, or crazy. Trying to appraise a situation by looking for cause-and-effect sequences often results in one-dimensional assumptions that are judgmental and that place blame.

Linear, cause-and-effect thinking

In the process of development, a young child needs to explore cause-and-effect sequences. She looks at the world from a concrete, egocentric point of view. She approaches life as if it were on a straight line and she were the starting point. From this perspective, she observes events and the cause-and-effect linkage between events. She discovers that walking in the street presents danger, that sharing her toys brings smiles, that climbing high can lead to big falls. She is the center of her experience, and she is learning some very important connections and relationships between parts of her world. She's discovering right and wrong, safe and unsafe. These are essential realities.

"Sesame Street" used to present, in its very early years, two wonderful characters named Buddy and Jim. These two went about exploring this very basic, linear relationship between things. Buddy would have a piece of cake in his hand, and he would wonder aloud whether he should open his mouth before or after he ate the cake. My kids tried to instruct him from their side of the TV set. Jim would carry a long piece of wood horizontally up to a doorway and experiment with how to get it through. Very important learning, very basic, a good way to solve practical problems.

There is a great deal more that goes on in life situations than what linear thinking and cause-and-effect sequences can account for. Interactions between persons are far more complex. However, for the sake of efficiency or from persevering in this early developmental mode, we often try to view interactions linearly. Kids come to parents to have them adjudicate who is right and wrong in an argument. Children believe in good guys and bad guys, and they believe parents are omnipotent. Fights between couples stalemate and accelerate over who is right and who is wrong. A couple may go to a therapist to seek a judgment. One of the partners may talk

> *The dialectic process uses the differences of each person's position and creates a synthesis that transcends both. Nothing and no one gets lost. One side doesn't have to yield or evaporate.*

to a friend or relative for confirmation that her/his position represents the "truth." It may seem efficient and just, or even scientific, to decipher a situation using linear, cause-and-effect thinking. Doing so makes one person right and the other wrong, or stupid, or crazy. Sometimes it makes one person the bad guy, and where there are bad guys there are victims. So then the position of being the good guy is secured through being the victim. Dangerous.

The dialectic process

There is a synergism lost, a dialectic process unable to unfold when the practical, linear mode prevails. The dialectic process is a generative one. It begins with statements of the positions of both sides, and it progresses to a synthesis that includes the important elements of each position. Each person has a different perspective in an encounter or interaction. No one perspective is the "true" one. The dialectic process uses the differences of each person's position and creates a synthesis that transcends both. Nothing and no one gets lost. One side doesn't have to yield or evaporate in order to make room for the other. Relationship implies two; when one side is relinquished, the result is loss of relationship. Complicity or monopoly is what the relationship turns into.

A two-year-old needs and deserves to have the chance to assert her own position. At this stage of her development, this is her life task. She's finding herself and drawing herself out of the symbiosis of infancy. The task in adult relationships is to become more distinct without dismissing the other person. Learning to retain one's own distinctness without destroying another's is the process by which intimacy develops. Intimacy is not achieved by one person's retreating to preserve the position of the other. Doing so leaves only one, and then closeness becomes the comfort of being unchallenged. For the very young child, this is an essential position to occupy. In adult interactions, it is narcissistic and immature.

Polarization from linear thinking

After a right/wrong debate, a retrenching takes place. In the effort to hold onto a position or after relinquishing it, each side re-embraces his/her original opinion. If one person wants to make a purchase and the other wants to save, whoever "wins" the right/wrong debate does so by out-arguing the other. If the purchaser is the "winner," his/her thoughts after the outcome may sound like, "What's money for, if not to get what you want and need?!" The saver will probably be looking for ways to save in other areas and how to resist the next expenditure. Each side becomes more dedicated to not being like the other. The partners become polarized. The emotional expression of one partner may stir up determination in the other to be more logical. And the increased rationality of the logical one will pull more emotion from the emotional one. Similarly, a careful, meticulous partner may become more so in the face of the other's disarray. The less orderly partner may react with more disorder to the insistence on perfection. Partners become increasingly opposite and reactive in the linear, right/wrong framework.

The consequences of the linear model become quite apparent at the level of society. Over issues like capital punishment and abortion, there is polarization. All those "for" line up against all those "opposed." And the debate goes on and on. Polarized, each side defames the other, attempting to destroy character and credibility. As the right/wrong rhetoric rages on, destroyed also are the opportunity to learn and the possibility of resolution, or at least, some advancement or amelioration of the issue.

This is dangerous and tragic: dangerous at the very least because where there are enemies, there is likely to be acceleration of warlike strategies; tragic at the very least because trust and the perspective of valuing each side is lost.

The struggle that takes place in a polarized marriage parallels the political posturing of Republicans and Democrats. A two-party political body often becomes divided and distrustful, unable to work together—filibustering instead. Opponents spend time and effort making points about the wrongness of the other's position, having abdicated responsibility for their own position. The largest, most tragic loss is that the process persons got married or were sent to Washington to get involved in never gets off the ground. The stage was set, the actors assembled, but the play never begins, much less has a chance to unfold.

Many marriages end without experiencing the dialectic of interaction. This awesome process makes sense out of conflict, promotes the development of each partner, and allows persons to reach conclusions and solutions that are a synergistic and catalytic mix of each that transcends both.

In my first position following my doctoral work, I was the outpatient therapist in a chemical dependency unit. When a soon-to-be outpatient entered detox, I would confer with the staff of that unit to arrive at case management decisions. The team consisted of the head nurse, the detox counselor, and myself. At times I felt strongly that my opinion should prevail; after all, I was the Ph.D. I almost missed the dialectic process, as I had innumerable times previously in my personal life. The nurse and the counselor were patient with my arrogance, and they didn't abdicate their own positions. Gradually we learned to evolve treatment plans that represented some of the best professional knowledge and experience of each of us. It was a very nice learning experience for me with these two fine people. They held onto themselves without overpowering me, and I learned to do the same. It was trustworthy, humbling, and very generative.

Transference: the "as if" trance

There is a mighty, though barely perceptible, trance that

takes place in interactions between persons. Understanding the intricacies of the trance goes a long way in helping to decipher and make sense of all that's going on in any interaction. In the trance, one functions "as if" things and persons are different from what they are. Psychologists call this "transference." In a professional therapeutic setting, transference is what occurs when the client begins to experience the therapist "as if" she or he were a significant person from the client's past. Feelings and attitudes that are actually about someone else in the client's life get attributed to the therapist. The process of transference can be very helpful in therapy if used well. Transference creates the opportunity for the client to reexperience feelings about important persons and events in her/his past. The client then has the chance to express the feelings and work out or finish some pieces of the past differently. A good therapist, who takes good care of her/his own needs outside the therapy room, will not get hooked by the transference. A responsible therapist will be able to recognize the client's transference and keep the boundaries safe, holding onto the present reality while exploring the past reality with the client. Transference doesn't occur only in professional therapy. Various characteristics in friends, lovers, strangers, business associates can trigger some emotions, and this trance-like transportation takes place. It is a trance that can get induced instantly, without our knowledge or cooperation.

The major professor in my doctoral program was a gentle

man. He was a very principled man. I chose him as my advisor throughout my graduate program. He was an excellent guide. He helped me get through, and he allowed me to experience a little more of my father at a time when my dad wasn't available to me. I was "transferred" in Dr. Higgins's presence. He was very much himself, and he didn't need or solicit my transference—that's some of what made it safe. There was a part of me that would walk into his office and learn more about what it meant to be fathered. That part of me was in a trance, was functioning "as if" Dr. Higgins were my dad. I didn't choose it to be so; it happened. It's only in retrospect, after more than a decade, that I realize it. Dr. Higgins could clarify the next step in climbing the Ph.D. mountain; he could spell out the academic requirements and standards. By his own personal manner, he spoke wordlessly of values and ethical standards. He provided a challenge each time, one that would stretch me without intimidating me. He seemed to have a sense of my capability to finish the doctoral program that I wasn't quite certain of yet. He is a fine man. He was a fine "father." At graduation he gave me my Ph.D. hood. Dr. Higgins is an "as if" father. I know it and I think he did too.

The "as if" trance and emotional intensity

The "as if" trance is one we can wander into and out of numerous times through a day. It is important to know that it happens and to become aware when it does. In fact, it can be very interesting to observe oneself in a trance and see what is happening. As with any hypnotic trance, there are often physiological clues which indicate a trance state. Pupils may dilate or constrict, breathing may slow or deepen, emotion may intensify. These are cues more easily observable in someone else. It can be helpful to assume that "as if" functioning is taking place when you observe increasing emotional intensity in another person. When, for instance, someone is raging, assuming that "as if" functioning is happening in that person will help to reinforce the notion that "it's not about me." Some of the same physiological signs can, with practice, be observed in oneself, especially the intensification of emotion.

When suddenly my call to the accounts department of a utility company has me involved in a to-the-death struggle with the customer service representative, something hypnotic has happened. Something in her manner strikes a chord with something deep in my viscera, and the trance is begun. A volcanic eruption starts there in my gut and rumbles up and spreads over me. I begin to tremble; my voice grows stronger and insistent. Without any consensual involvement on my part, she has become my mother, and I am now fourteen years old, fighting once again for some credibility with her. It is useless.

It is not the service representative's job to give me credit for my integrity. I suspect my insistence has set off some part of her past experience. So now we are both in a trance, each having been transported away from the here and now to some time in the past. We are both functioning "as if" we are each someone else for the other. Frustrated and irate, I get off the phone. She is the most obnoxious person I ever met! How did she get hired as a customer service representative? She is wrong and stupid and crazy!

In one simple interaction between persons who will never cross paths again, an amazing, complex process has unfolded. In a matter of minutes this woman, unknown to me, reached into the core of my unconscious, visceral experience. She allowed me to reexperience an essential drama of my life. I have done the same for her. And neither of us had the intention to do so or gave consent to the doing or the being done to. How helpful this re-creation could be, but how infuriating the situation is if this fascinating interplay is overlooked. Somewhere along the way, during countless interactions that begin as nothing more than they are, the house lights dim and the stage lights come on. The scene is transformed. The interplay between the actors re-creates a drama within each.

Jean and Christie's interplay

Jean and Christie are involved in an interplay. Jean is a high school English teacher. She is a very conscientious woman who works hard to provide enriching experiences for her students.

Christie is a multi-talented student, recognized by her teachers as showing exceptional promise. Jean is particularly enthusiastic about the opportunity to teach Christie. In fact, she considers her responsibility to be greater in the guidance of such a student. Christie, in spite of her academic capabilities, is more interested in establishing herself with her friends than in meeting her teacher's lofty expectations. Jean and Christie meet simply as teacher and student in the classroom. The stage lights are about to go on, however. Christie's seeming indifference becomes a challenge to Jean, who puts even more effort into her classroom preparation. Her student's indifference hooks Jean and begins to become a measure of Jean's success or failure as a teacher. One side of the stage is transformed. To Christie, Jean's interest and expectations become, at first, a burden she seeks to avoid. As Jean's efforts escalate, Christie begins to get a message about herself that would surprise her teacher: "What I'm doing is not good enough; I'm not good enough." The other side of the stage is lit.

> *We dance with each other to music that resonates from early emotional strains. The footwork was choreographed years before.*

45

One day the teacher's exasperation meets the student in the hall between classes. Jean wants to know why Christie is quiet and withdrawn in class. The younger woman's "not-good-enough" bell begins to ring. Teacher begins to detail what she has done to intrigue student, all to no avail. Jean's frustration is gilded with her need to not fail with such a promising student. As the interaction escalates, Christie's bell tolls louder: "I'm not good enough." There is much pain and anger in that experience, and it spills out in Christie's remarks as she exits the hallway, stage left. Jean is alone now on center stage, alone with her self-doubts. Christie's gut-wrenching experience of "nothing I do is good enough" can be set aside if she focuses on her teacher's behavior. She can dispel her own painful feelings by making critical remarks to her friends about Jean. She'll have to say many critical things to get rid of all the pain. Jean has her peers in the teachers' lounge to talk to if she decides to exorcize her self-doubt by getting worked up over how spoiled and immature Christie appeared. The stage lights have dimmed, and the opportunity to learn about self is disappearing. The possibility of understanding what the interaction has been about is fading too.

For Christie, the stage was set to learn more about the worthless feeling that plagues her in spite of her talents. Christie's story involves having been adopted into her family. Being a chosen child in this family to Christie means having been discarded by another. There may be a lot of things in Christie's life that don't make sense to the naked eye. The feeling of being not-good-enough-to-keep that haunts her will create many dramas, each an invitation to wrestle with the roots of her arrival in the world. No wonder that where she fits with her friends is important to her.

Jean's play-within-the-play is about a girl who grew up longing for the guidance she now seeks to provide. She knows how essential the availability of a concerned adult is to a young person. She knows how devastating the absence of that availability is. She must not fail. If she does fail, her aloneness is confirmed once again.

Being aware of the trance

In interactions like Jean and Christie's, we dance with each other to music that resonates from early emotional strains. The footwork of the dance we each do was choreographed years before and, even if we are strangers, we cue each other's steps as though we are familiar partners. The trance that "as if" induces allows hypnotic, robotic behavior to play out. As entranced actors in the interplay, we reach unknowingly into each other's guts. We touch things we have no idea we have touched. We walk away from each other having huge chunks of our own stuff swimming in our guts, oblivious to what it is that we stirred in the other.

We need not remain entranced. The spell can be broken. One

or both of us can return to conscious awareness. It is fascinating to discover oneself in a trance, to walk around in that world, to learn about it, and to call oneself back to the present, having brought along the entranced experience. It would be like diving deep into the ocean, retrieving an object from that world, and bringing it up to the surface and onto the shore, there having the opportunity to handle and scrutinize the object. This back-to-the-past transportation happens whether we know it or not. Acknowledging that it happens and when it happens allows one to examine "objects" from his/her previous world. As we each begin to make sense out of our own experience, we begin to develop a foundation on which our relationships with others can stand.

Chapter three

External Focus: Recognizing Reactive Cycles, Meaning-Making, Self-Abandonment

The search for relationship is persistent over the life span. The yearning for relationship is so strong that we are willing to withstand much trial and tribulation in the pursuit. Relationships with family, friends, mentors, lovers, coworkers, and colleagues are a great part of the joy and vitality of life. Relationships are challenging. It takes intricate and delicate maneuvering to navigate the course of establishing and developing them, while preserving self and honoring the other.

Much that occurs in relationship is devastating to the persons involved and is not about relating at all. Relating is about mutuality, regard, and communion. If the potential relaters are stuck in a linear conceptualization of interaction and if they have been taught that their value is directly proportional to what others think of them, then the prospect for real relationship is very dismal. But the yearning for relationship is persistent. So, many step onto the treadmill of trying. Some are successful at taking captives, others at being captives. Yet even the certainty of defeat has possibilities. The defeat can highlight what is missing and what the next step might be. The experience of attempting relationship from a linear, my-value-depends-on-approval point of view offers roadblocks that encourage development of what is missing.

There are many ways of bonding between two persons, many vital, loving forms that relationship takes. I have spent a great deal of time living in a marriage, working on me in it, and with him in it. The focus of my work as a therapist has been marriage and the family. Marriage is the relationship that I have chosen to discuss here. I hope that it may serve as a reference from which applications to other relationships can be made.

Marriage and the "as if" interplay

The married couples and the divorced and widowed persons who attend a wedding are the ones who know. They may not have all the answers, but they are familiar with the territory of a marriage. They remember the days of magic, from the moment of encounter that transformed their experience to the early passage through the world of lovers: the meeting of souls, the experience of being wanted and pursued, the availability of the other, the growing closeness, the excitement and anticipation of time spent together, the discovery of much to value and love, the feeling of being valued and loved. They also know that the splendor and celebration of the wedding day usher the couple into a new territory. There is a glow that spreads and stays a while. But, almost immediately, the glow gets pierced by the interplay, that dynamic interaction between the two. The interplay takes on a new dimension on the other side of marriage.

Marriage initiates Act Two of the lover drama. In the second act, the "as if" interplay becomes more complex because the number of dimensions has increased. As the bond and commitment between the lovers increase, a new family begins. The experience in the new family amplifies the family-of-origin resonance for each spouse. As soon as the marriage begins, it is stressed to evolve from the romantic symbiosis that created it. The amplified interplay happens occasionally at first, interrupting the glow momentarily and revealing some rough terrain. The glow is reestablished fairly easily, and the rough terrain of the marriage territory recedes from view. Eventually, it is the glow that returns only occasionally if the newlyweds don't find out what to do with the intensified interplay.

Those persons experienced for some years with the terrain of marriage know how the very quality that endeared begins to irritate. They also know the disillusion and disappointment. They could empathize with the young bride who will feel abandoned or betrayed at times by the young man who has just pledged his fidelity. They could have compassion when the young man feels alone with some responsibility and wonders where his helpmate is. They know those moments well. They know the disbelief that accompanies those moments, yet they hold up the dream like a carrot and wish the young couple all the happiness in the world. There is much collective knowledge among them, the experienced ones, that the young couple could learn from.

As the glow becomes fragile, the newlyweds will wonder what's wrong with him, or her, or us? It is not working. All the happiness in the world is elusive. What happened to the closeness, the excitement, the valuing? The marriage and spouse can begin to look like the problem, and when that happens, someone else can easily become the solution. And the pursuit of the dream continues.

When there is not much relationship within before there is relationship between, the devastation that results will have embedded within it all the clues for developing that internal relationship.

There is so much going on; there is so much to be talked about. The dream of happiness cannot be attained without deep experience on the rough roads that marriage takes the couple down. Those of us experienced in and weathered by those roads could be more honest with the newlyweds. We could be useful to them if we were willing to acknowledge that our journey with each other has taken us to the depths of our own personal despair. That there were times, some lasting weeks or months, we were hopeless, confused, or in pain. That the way you get to all the happiness in the world is through the depths of your own despair. One cannot be avoided, or the other will not be attained.

If the days preceding the wedding were busy and hectic, there is no less going on after the honeymoon. Once the wedding "we" is established, the urge to separate becomes the next most pressing need. It's like the tide; as soon as it comes in, it must go out in order to come in again. The "we" creates the need to recover the "I," so that the "we" can be embraced again. It is natural and it is essential. One condition creates the need for the other. The process is also like hunger. Hunger creates the search for food, which results in energy that can be spent. And the spending is all the while creating the next hunger. The "we-I" cycle is inherent in relationship. How easy it is, however, to experience the search for separateness as abandonment.

"Looking for Mr./Mrs. Good Parent"

It is especially easy since the state of marriage induces the "Looking for Mr. or Mrs. Good Parent" trance. "As if" comes running up the aisle and transports the bride and groom back to childhood. Will this love be the one that never fails, is unconditional, and is ever present? I don't think so, but that is the expectation of the trance. Parent and lover/spouse get intermingled.

Traditional roles enhance the Good Parent trance. When men allocate an allowance and give special gifts, women can slip into being little girls with their daddies. When women pick out husband's clothes and decide what they will eat, men can slip into being little boys with their mommies. The roles themselves aren't bad, and some of these actions feel very loving. Getting captured by the Good Parent trance and not knowing it, is what creates the disappointment and estrangement.

In marriage we sign up to be each other's lover, not each other's parent. Parents don't make love with their children; it is devastating if that kind of intimacy, either emotional and/or sexual, exists between parents and children. If we marry and don't know when we slip into trying to find the Good Parent, the intimacy we married with and the glow it brings will erode. Our lover will distance herself/himself, not knowing it is the role of parent she/he is resisting, only knowing how smothering it feels. When a lover refuses to be parent, a person can reexperience childhood abandonment. Learning how to recognize the Good Parent trance when one is in it becomes essential to the survival of the relationship and to the growth of the individual.

"Am I a Keeper?"

Another trance is "Am I a Keeper?" In the best of circumstances, even before a child can or does ask the question, the adults around are conveying to the child the beauty they see in her. As we talk to the infant, our eyes and face say you are incredible, engaging, amazing, and wonderful. Children learn to look up to check the reaction on adult faces as they show us more and more about themselves. How am I doing? Is this OK? Do you still love me even though I got so mad?

The child's questions are about her very existence and her being. Huge issues. She needs to find out that she can safely stay with these adults, that she is free to experience herself and try new ways to learn and grow. Each time she looks up, she needs to find in the eyes of the adult that she is still amazing and OK, even if what she just did is not.

Marriage exposes all our ways and parts to each other. Our beloved sees how we act when exhausted and under pressure, when frightened, and when we are vulnerable and sick. All our reflexive reactions, family ways, and personal foibles eventually are exposed. "What do you think of me now? Am I still safe with you? Am I still valued?" It is the search for acknowledgement of one's essence. We have to know if we are a "Keeper."

The new spouses who are busy reestablishing their "I" positions also need to be able to discern when they are entranced, so they can keep Good Parent separate from lover and find Keeper safety within the marriage. That's a lot going on, not to mention careers, in-laws, finances, children, etc. The longing for intimate relationship is great, as are the challenges inherent in it.

Other-contingent orientation and external focus

There are some places we can get stuck in that withhold the possibility of successful intimate relating and enlarge the longing for it. One of these places is the orientation to the world that locates self by means of the other. This other-contingent orientation makes self-worth dependent upon the approval of others and forms behavioral choices in reaction to others. External focus is the chief characteristic of this other-contingent orientation. External focus prevents intimate relating because it sets up abdication of self. This other-contingent orientation produces persons who choose submission as well as persons who choose a powerful role in relationships. External focus develops qualities and skills that are very useful and desirable in this society, among them responsibility, endurance, sensitivity to others, and perfectionism, to name a few. Persons who are successful in other areas of their lives may have a very difficult time in relationship if they are externally focused and other-oriented.

When children look to the face of another for affirmation, they are discovering their being and learning how to remember that they are somebody. They are building their internal power source. When, as adults, our eyes look to the face of another for affirmation of our being, there is a power shift. The power shifts from an internalized sense of self to an externalized sense of self. A good, old, well-researched psychological variable is Locus of Control. The theory states that if our locus of control is external, there are powerful others in our lives who have more of the power and control than we do. On the other hand, if our locus of control is internal, we have more power relative to our lives than others have with us. I am used to referring to this concept as "internal focus and external focus." I prefer the term "focus" because it has a tangible counterpart in our physiology. Whether focus is internal or external can be determined by checking where our eyes are directed. Becoming aware of where we are focusing is a way to detect if a power shift has taken place. When our eyes are riveted on the other, personal power can be given away. It happens without the conscious cooperation of either person.

External focus is a natural part of a child's experience. The child must reference others to discover herself. When a parent holds his infant child in his arms, the child is able to begin to distinguish herself and her body from her parent's. The holding surrounds her with that which she is not, and she begins to experience the difference. The parent holding the child is, for me, a powerful metaphor that tells much about relationships. As the child is cradled by the arms and chest of the parent, she is able to experience the safety and joy of the symbiotic "we." She is, at the same time, offered the opportunity to begin to discover who she is and who she is not. She bumps into the difference as she is being held. Through millions of variations of this bumping into another, the child defines her "I," which allows her to eventually enjoy a "we" that is not so symbiotic. Some of the bumping is wonderful, and a good deal of it is difficult or painful.

The process of referencing others as a means of discovering self may be thought of as developmental external focus. Theoretically, a child would use external focus less and less as her internal sense of self grows. Ideally, as adults, we would need to reference others only to relocate ourselves. When we become dizzy or lose equilibrium, it is reflexive to look outside ourselves to reestablish balance and a sense of self in relation to the environment. But very frequently, long past childhood, persons still use external focus as the principal means of building an internal sense of self and power source.

Prolonged external focus—from unpredictability and imperfect parenting

Prolonged use of external focus results from a number of variables; unpredictability is one of them. If a child lives where there is much unpredictability, she will of necessity be externally focused. It's somewhat like concentrating. If you are working on a project like solving a problem or writing a letter, your focus is very much close in to you. If there are many distractions, like loud music, someone trying to talk to you, the phone ringing, or a thunderstorm, your close, internal focus will be broken repeatedly and will be pulled outside or externalized. Examples of unpredictability in a child's environment are sudden disruptions like someone's temper exploding, the death or prolonged absence of a parent, moving, and sickness. Other kinds of unpredictability include changes that take place in a variable or arbitrary way, such as mood changes, inconsistencies in rules and discipline, and lapses in emotional contact. Any kind of dishonesty or withholding of information can also make the environment unpredictable for a child. Environments with alcoholism in them are not the only places unpredictability resides.

Prolonged external focus results also from imperfect parenting. Sounds like blasphemy, but maybe that's just part of the definition of parenting—being imperfect. As soon as we all catch our breath again, we can explore that idea. It's the same as speaking of dysfunction in families, a concept perhaps not quite so shocking. Many people are willing to say they come from dysfunctional families. Few are willing to say their kids are growing up in one. I believe dysfunction is as much a part of families as functionality is. Talking about it and being willing to own up to the dysfunction is the first step to increased functionality. I think we have to get over the idea that we aren't dysfunctional.

Back to imperfect parenting. Parenting is such an important

job—immense responsibility with no respite. There is no professional training for it. And most of us begin parenting before we are very grown up ourselves. In fact, parenting is a great and continued catalyst for one's own growth. So how could anyone be perfect at parenting? Therefore—imperfect parenting. That's not a perfect syllogism either, but perhaps it is sufficient to introduce the concept of imperfect parenting.

Because parenting is imperfect, there may be missing pieces in a child's development—few or very many, little ones or big ones. When, as an adult, we have detected ourselves to be in a moment (or much more than a moment) of external focus, we have probably come to a place where something is missing. That same moment and place create the opportunity to fill in the gap. "As if" has probably shown up again, and some kind of trance is transforming the experience and setting the stage. How helpful if we know what to do with the trance.

Reactive cycles

First, it may be helpful to have an idea of what external focus does to us. As the power shifts from internal to external, we become reactive. When a very bright light shines directly in my eyes, I react reflexively. Pupils constrict, eyes squint, and head tries to dodge the light. The light is in charge of what I will do. Of course, the light doesn't know it's in charge. It's the same in an interaction in which one person has become externally focused on the other. That person is reacting to the other; the other is in charge of what the first person will do, though the other has no idea how powerful she/he has become. If the other becomes externally focused also, a reactive cycle begins.

When both persons become externally focused, interaction between them escalates, because they have become reactive to each other. With each verbal exchange, more reaction is provoked and the interaction continues to intensify. The two become caught in a vicious cycle that closes in on both. Once reaction sets in, communication stops. What happens during whatever comes next goes nowhere. Reactive cycles control, disorient, and exhaust. Reactive cycles make lovers feel like enemies and cause wars to develop between parents and children. Reactive cycles initiate power struggles. No one can win; each person just gets devastated and desperate.

The reactive cycle: a personal story

A very interesting thing happens between my husband and myself. It starts very quietly as I begin to say something I feel or want. It seems quiet to me anyway. There is a part of me that believes my husband welcomes hearing my feelings even if it involves telling him about something he did. In my fantasy it would go like this: "Did you know you stepped on my foot a moment ago? It really hurt." He would say, "Oh, honey, did I? Gosh, I didn't even realize it. Are you OK?" Having been heard,

I would look tenderly at him and we could touch in some way, a pat or hand squeeze. Nice.

Not what happens. In an instant, we both can become externally focused and then reactive. I begin, "Honey, I felt uncomfortable when you...." I usually start with my feeling and then slip into talking more about what he did. I scan for what the effect of my comment is. There is the first major shift. I started with me, slipped into talking about him, and then scanned his reaction. Bo's trance initiates when he hears my words as an attack. For years I lived with him and did not know that happened. I had no idea that he experienced the expression of my feelings as an attack. The effect of my comment registers on his face; I pick it up and begin reacting to it. I believe he is irritated with me, and I also believe that he wouldn't be if he understood what I am trying to say. So my reaction involves trying harder to explain what I meant. And he feels more of an attack. I can try harder for a very long time! Something in me insists that I try harder—it's very painful for me to be both misunderstood and not responded to. As my insistence and effort grow, so does Bo's feeling of being attacked, and the reactive cycle is full blown. We have escalated and there is no place to go from here, no winning, no understanding. We don't even realize what has happened. We do now, of course. But it took what felt like a million of those escalating "go-nowhere" cycles and some very good therapy to decipher what was happening. Countless times we seemed like enemies to each other.

Through those countless crashes into our own and each other's trances, we have finally learned a great deal about ourselves and each other. I needed to learn that trying harder was not going to make it better. It's amazing to me now to see how many cues I would ignore and push past. I believed Bo's reaction was all about me, so I never stopped and asked what was going on with him. My persistence is a very useful quality, but it can also get me into a lot of trouble.

The "gears" of relationship

I have this image of two gears that run according to mechanisms that are different and unique to each. As the gears come closer together, their spoked wheels must synchronize in a way that allows both to keep moving autonomously and without grinding as they move together. I think persons are like the two unique gears. The challenge of relationship is to learn how to keep the gears turning together without loss of uniqueness and without smashing into each other so severely that the gears are maimed. When gears grind, it's important to stop and sort out what's happening. One gear or the other is not bad or useless. Each is fascinating and unique, and each may be enhanced and have greater function if the challenge is met.

When the gears grind, a mechanic has to look at each and determine certain characteristics of the movement of each at different points along the arc of the turn. In other words, if the unified turning of the gears is to be achieved, the uniqueness of each has to be separated out and understood before turning resumes. If we can anthropomorphize the gears to give them intelligence, some concern and, perhaps, love for each other, the gears may want to understand what's going on with each other so they could devise a way to turn together. Again, a reminder of the importance of each "I" in the creation of a "we."

"Speaking from my presumptions about you"

In addition to reactive cycles, another convolution of communication that ensues from external focus and interferes seriously with the resolution of gear grinding is what I call "speaking from my presumptions about you." When my focus slips off me and onto you, I begin gathering data on you and knowing much more about what you are doing than what I am doing. As soon as I start talking after my focus slips, I'll be talking about you. I'll be able to tell you all kinds of details about what you are doing; I'll also know what you should be doing. And most likely I'll tell you. You become the subject of my sentences. Since you didn't request all this wonderful information, you probably won't appreciate receiving it. You may feel defensive against or angry at my arrogance. Of course, I don't think I'm being arrogant; I'm problem-solving and trying to be helpful.

There is much pain and loss in this simple switch of perspective. Boundaries are invaded. Twelve-Step programs call it taking someone else's inventory. We know we shouldn't but we do, and sometimes we speak of it. It happens easily, automatically. But it is a very serious invasion with very large consequences. I, having become an authority on you in some highly specific detail, begin to make judgments and recommendations. It is offensive—and would seem more so if it weren't so routine in our experience. It's your territory, your life, your experience; I can't even walk in it. I can only view it from my territory. And I become twisted like a pretzel when trying to be a voyeur of some part of your territory. So what I think I know is extremely limited, yet I speak with such authority. What power we assume with another and how we feel right and just in doing so, even benevolent in our helping.

The abusiveness and invasion are not the only consequences of speaking from my presumptions about you. Escalation is another. Interactions will become increasingly intense and reactive. Defensiveness and anger are understandable reactions to such invasion. But because I am being so helpful, I'll be offended by your defensiveness and anger. Our reactions to each other will begin piling up. I'll walk away from the reactive, escalated interaction and believe I know even more about you. If you weren't so sensitive and angry all the time, things would go better for you. I can hardly say anything to you without your getting upset!

There is yet another consequence of the perspective switch that is less obvious but no less devastating to both the invader and the relationship. This is the complete loss of the original, unique perspective and feelings of the invader. By staying in my shoes but twisting to get the scoop on you, I have abdicated whatever my awareness of myself was. Not only have I made a sham of your experience, but I have annihilated my own. There is precious information lost. You may not want to know this information, but I need to know it. What was my feeling that initiated my perspective twist? I need to know so I can respond to me, rather than react to you. And if I am important to you, you may want to know also.

I remember a family that was struggling with issues of adolescence and independence. The father was insisting that his son give one day's advance notice if he wanted to use the car for any purpose. The father was presenting a great deal of evidence of his son's lack of responsibility and planning. The son was arguing that it would not always be possible to know twenty-four hours in advance, and that it seemed controlling and arbitrary for his father to insist on such notice. The interaction was escalating, with much frustration and distance increasing on both sides. When asked if he could say what he was feeling while presenting the evidence, the father responded, "Sometimes I feel used." Precious information. The father needed to know what he was feeling so he could discover how to help himself. The expression of the feeling created a wonderful opportunity for the family to know more about the man who was fathering them. The son was quite responsive to his dad. He was amazed to learn that his dad wasn't speaking from a need to control but from a need to protect himself.

The entire interaction changed. The son appreciated and respected this honest expression of his dad's feelings. It was a very special moment. After expressing himself and receiving such a response from his son, the father was able to listen to his son's feelings and point of view. Together they arrived at a solution that honored them both.

Meaning-making

Meaning-making is another phenomenon which results from external focus and which helps to drive reactive cycles.

In an environment where sufficient information is lacking, a child has to guess about meanings and connections. In order to grasp what is going on, the child has to fill in or make up information. If something abrupt or tense is going on in the home and no one is talking about it, the child will have to assign some meaning. It doesn't matter if the information is correct or not; it feels better to a child to have the gaps filled. Ever since coming into this world, a child has been oriented to making sense of it. She takes bits of this and that and goes about sorting, categorizing, associating, fitting the bits into an organized whole. In time, language forms as well as a knowledge base about a great many things. If some bits are lacking, and especially if the situation presents some urgency, the child will assign meaning to make a whole.

Andy's story: meaning-making

Our oldest son told us, many years later, about his perception of an event that happened in our home. It was after dinner, and seven-year-old Andy had gone upstairs to play in his room. His father and I began arguing while we cleared the table. As the argument escalated, Andy came down the stairs to see what was going on. He remembers seeing me kneeling by the table, wiping something up. I was crying. Andy thought it was my teeth that I was gathering up from the floor. He thought his father had hit me and my teeth had fallen out. Bo and I have argued many times; he has never hit me. It didn't happen, but to Andy it had happened. He told us he went to his room and tried to decide what to do. His decision was that if I didn't stop crying, he was going to call Uncle Jim. What a good decision that was. Uncle Jim would have been an excellent helper.

It was rice I was wiping up. We had rice a lot in those early years. Andy put a number of cues together: the arguing, my crying, and the urgency he felt. He assigned meaning to the white stuff on the floor. The other cues helped him decide what the white stuff was. He made a whole out of the parts he experienced and decided what to do based on his information. His systems were working overtime, and they were working well. I have a lot of empathy for that little boy. He was scared. I wonder how many times each of our children was in a situation that seemed scary or overwhelming to them and we had no idea.

Whenever there isn't sufficient information concerning one of the variables in a situation, the opportunity to make meaning exists. Over the years a person may develop considerable "skill." In fact, meaning-making often becomes a major part of one's coping style. We may be very proud of our ability to meaning-make: "I can pick up on what people are feeling," "I know why he did that," "She wants to intimidate me." It is tempting. It is seemingly efficient to meaning-make. Why should I bother to inquire about that which I already think I know? Anyway, why put so much effort into simple interactions? Because it's amazing how complex simple interactions become without the effort of inquiring.

Sam and Emma's story: meaning-making

One afternoon in a therapy session, a couple in their seventies uncovered some meaning-making that had been going on for a number of years. Emma had felt hurt each time Sam would clear his throat, turn his head, and raise his eyebrows a certain way. To Emma, this behavioral sequence had always meant that Sam was disgusted with what she had just said or done. Sam had been unconscious of his gestures and unaware of the feelings they stirred in Emma. The sequence occurred during the session that afternoon. Sam was amazed when he heard the meaning Emma had made all those years. Though unaware of his gestures, Sam was able to name the feeling he was having. That sequence of reflexive movements occurred when he felt awkward or embarrassed. There was silence as each received the other's information. Their eyes traced the air as though reviewing, in a moment, their considerable history. Wordlessly, understanding was exchanged as the tracing stopped and their eyes met. Suddenly I felt like an intruder in this beautiful, now very private experience.

How often and in how many relational settings does a similar devastating dance take place? Some random pieces of behavior occur and become laden with meaning. The next time the behavior occurs, it's as though a scientifically controlled experiment has taken place. The original hypothesis is now proven, with no allowance for error of measurement. Repetition elevates theory to fact, and slowly it all becomes part of the history of the relationship.

Meaning-making between parents and children

Parents of an infant develop considerable skill at discerning subtle differences in cries that call for food, sleep, or changing. As the child grows, she becomes infinitely more complex, and yet frequently parents still believe they can "read" their teenager. When she tosses her head and slings her keys on the counter, the parents know what that means. When he slams the door and blasts his music, they know. This kind of knowing often begins to create a prison within which parents and young people struggle. It is a prison because the meanings made are as solid as iron bars and such certainty attaches to the meanings that they become inescapable. It's a horrible bind that each side has the other in.

Parents may decide that their child is a manipulator and then set about showing the child the reality of this fact, hoping to impress upon her the need to change. The young person may feel judged, hounded, or not trusted. She may begin to react out of those feelings and produce behavior that may strengthen the parents' case. The parents' fear will subside if their child sees herself as they see her and if she begins to change what they perceive to be her problem. If she takes this on, the young person must abdicate her own reality and begin to behave so as to relieve her parents' anxiety.

The young person may decide that her parents don't care about her. She may believe they would care if she were different than she is. Once she embraces this belief, the young person may no longer be able to see the signs of caring that come from her parents. The sides are divided, each reacting to the other based on "certain" but twisted knowledge of each other. Communication has ceased, though there may be an incredible number of powerful words that hang in the air. The verbiage that goes back and forth is the speaking-out-of-my-presumptions-about-you kind. People begin nailing each other in an attempt to prove that they are right.

The meanings we make are almost always wrong. Once made, however, the made-up meaning becomes the "truth" and is incredibly resistant to any evidence to the contrary. We begin to see each other through the lens of our made-up reality, discarding information that doesn't fit our view and incorporating that which does. The meanings we make up lock and bind, as over the years the evidence continues to pile up. "He has no feelings." "She thinks she's better than anyone else."

If all this begins due to insufficient information, it doesn't always stop when the missing information is supplied. Sometimes, family members are locked into the made-up reality. It is a very egocentric position, usually fueled by fear and hurt. Very many times I have seen members of a family willing to hear and incorporate the information that was missing. Those are loving, responsive, relieving experiences. In order for that to happen, persons must be willing to entertain the notion that how it has seemed to them may not be the way it is.

Self-abandonment and potential for abuse

The externalized focus used by a child to build an internal power source has devastating consequences when used by an adult. Instead of building an internalized sense of self, external focus sets up abdication of self. The possibility of relationship diminishes while the longing for relationship becomes more insistent and urgent. Living in reaction to others and repeating reactive cycles take an abundant toll. Reactiveness increases anxiety and fear, and calls for more control of self and others. Reactive cycles infuriate and devastate. Distrust grows and hopefulness diminishes. Sense of self begins to erode, as convoluted communication patterns and fabricated realities intensify and predominate. More sense of self is relinquished as externalized focus on others replaces awareness of one's own needs and feelings. Living in reaction to others and becoming nonresponsive to self demolish self-respect and create a vast accumulation of frustration. The unmet needs and feelings pave the way for compulsive acting out, the compulsions issuing further devastating blows to the self. The need-hunger that results may be experienced as feelings of

Living in reaction to others demolishes self-respect, increases anxiety and fear, diminishes hopefulness, sets up abdication of self. Unmet needs and feelings pave the way for compulsive acting out.

73

failure, vulnerability, and fragility. Or the need-hunger, though huge, may be masked by feelings of power and control. Self-abandonment and need-hunger create the potential for abuse.

Needs and feelings must be met and expressed. They will be met and expressed covertly if denied conscious, responsible means of expression. Compulsions expedite covert expression, and compulsions also become anesthetic for needs and feelings. It is this need-hungry, self-abdicated state that allows one person to act out on another. External focus does not create an internal power source for adults; it creates self-abandonment and establishes the condition that permits one to abuse or be abused.

I intentionally use the term "abuse" loosely, out of the sense that it is important to uncover abuse and the potential for it. Abuse is not just about cigarette burns and violent beatings. Abuse is happening when a mom or dad yells at or hits kids out of their own frustration or embarrassment. Abuse is happening when a teacher's exhaustion and edginess are taken out in impatience with a child. Abuse is happening when a helping professional has such a great need to feel competent that she/he becomes overly involved with a client. If we think of the possibility of abuse only in the extreme, we remove ourselves from the possibility of committing it. Understanding the continuum of abuse and the origins of the subtle end of the continuum allows personal intervention on the larger abuses found in twentieth-century society.

The defeat and devastation we feel when attempting relationship from the linear, externally focused perspective create the opportunity for us to collide with what is missing. Relationship with others depends on the breadth and depth of the relationship with ourselves. When there is not much relationship *within* before there is relationship *between*, the devastation that results will have embedded within it all the clues and roadmaps for developing that internal relationship. All our previous life experience, from family of origin to the present, will be needed in the pursuit. Fortunately, our stories, rich in detail, are embedded inside our bodies. Emotions will allow us to explore the depths of our own stories, and emotions will allow the development of relatedness within.

Chapter four

Emotional Knowing: Using the Hologram to Access Emotional Memory and Change Beliefs

I was waiting for the elevator in a renovated older building. Old brick and artifacts surrounded me: stained glass, framed mirrors, well-worn handrails. These things had obviously been salvaged from other buildings and reassembled here. It all created a comfortable air. I was lost in thought. Realizing I had been waiting awhile, I looked up for some indication that the elevator was coming. My eyes found a very old, very familiar object— an up-down indicator, yellowed, pre-electronic—and I was transported to another place and time. Suddenly I was shorter and it was higher. I was a little girl, eight to ten years old, looking up at it, standing by my mother's side. Pieces of feelings and memories accompanied the experience: little white gloves, a blue coat with velvet buttons, cold legs, the physical presence of my mother, a sense of her comfort in a world new to me. Were we at Lasalle's, where the elevators had bells and the operators called the floors and goods at each stop? Or were we about to be whisked into my dad's world of quiet carpets, big desks, lots of papers, and tall men in dark suits? Images of early experiences, yes, but also reexperiencing those early experiences. The elevator arrived, and I left the little girl and her mother.

Powerful transportation. And a powerful faculty we possess, this ability to reexperience through our senses. The memories that thunder forth I call "emotional memories." They are packed with sensual detail and emotional resonance. I like to think of the emotional memory as the location of our first knowing. A baby experiences the world through her senses, engulfing and incorporating the world through her eyes, mouth, fingers. She stores immense amounts of information before she has the capacity for verbal, conscious brain memory. Certainly her brain is involved in the sorting and storing of the information. But I believe that there is a separate, primary way of experiencing and learning about the world that needs to be distinguished from the verbal capacity that is schooled in us. Verbal capacity gets so much attention and training and is exalted as the proof of intelligence. I believe that the emotional way of learning is the seat of our intelligence and that it is primary—the first kind of knowing to come and the kind that stays until we go.

A four-month-old baby knows much about the valuing and smiling that pass from her parents to herself. As she receives the warmth and love of her parents, her hands come together and there is a physical response in the middle of her little body. There is a contraction in her solar plexus that looks like the point of impact where the valuing coming from her mom's and dad's eyes is registered. Her senses receive the experience of being loved. She "knows" it. Her brain is involved in the knowing, but certainly it's not the brain's verbal part. She is born with a knowing and a storage capacity that is powerful. That doesn't go away or yield to a higher form of knowing; it feeds and underwrites the verbal form.

Emotional knowing: a story about my father

I had an amazing experience with my father just weeks before his death. He had Alzheimer's disease. It was very advanced and had torn away in pieces my father's verbal intelligence. He had long since stopped reading the *Wall Street Journal* and no longer knew our names. During one of my visits, he had been touching my watch as I stood at his bedside. The word "clock" came out, accompanied by a furtive look. I went to his dresser and brought his watch and keys to him. The watch slid up to his elbow, and he fingered the keys. Objects familiar, but purpose gone. During another visit several months later, after my dad had been speechless for some time, we were alone in the room. I was unable to hold back some pain I was experiencing. My father's eyes showed concern as he saw my tears come. I began to tell him about the struggle I was having with my husband. I spoke of my fear and hurt as I cried. This man, who could no longer speak, looked tenderly at me and reached out his hands to hold my face and wipe at the tears. What a precious moment. This was an amazing gift to me, his love and comfort delivered in an old, familiar way. He was no longer verbally intelligent, but his emotional knowing was clearly present.

In the spaces where there aren't chairs, buildings, trees, cars, or people, there are the echoes of every day before this one.

Accessing the emotional memory data base

As this primary emotional knowing accumulates and is stored, it becomes a powerful and rich data base. Information is encoded, not verbally, but colorfully, symbolically, sensually. Details, sounds, smells, experiential knowledge of relationships and principles—of everything that we've ever experienced. All of this is accessible if we are willing to experience our emotions.

I believe that the denial of feelings is what blocks access to this awesome data base. In our culture, being in a feeling state has become equated with being out of control. Giving priority to composure and control means learning how to block and deny feelings and, therefore, pulling the plug on our connection to the immense storage system of emotional memory. Once the connection is broken and after many subsequent disconnections, the data base seems not to exist, and we continue to function apparently without needing its essential information. This way of functioning reminds me of an inebriated person who drives a car in a blackout. The brain stem is doing the driving, while the cerebral cortex is anesthetized. The more often someone drives "successfully" in a blackout, the more he/she develops a confidence about driving with the brain stem. Living and making decisions without access to all the experiences that form our knowledge base seem to me just as frightening as driving with only a brain stem.

Coping mechanisms of shock and dissociation

When the impact of an event is too large, one of several coping mechanisms may intervene. Physiological and psychological shock keep the body and the psyche from feeling the full impact of a trauma. The trauma is making its mark on the body or psyche, but, mercifully, the immense feelings, though registering, are not being felt.

Dissociation is another coping skill that protects. It is a more severe disconnection and not as transient as shock. An event that results in dissociation is recorded in emotional memory, but consciousness of the event is severed. Retrieval of the dissociated consciousness provides an example of how emotional memory functions. A child who witnesses an act of violence may need to split his consciousness in order to survive the experience. Otherwise, the violence would probably overwhelm his senses and his ability to comprehend. As he witnesses an event from a category previously unknown to him, he may feel as threatened as he would if the assault were happening to him. Each detail of the event will be received through his senses and registered on his brain. The threat and immensity of the experience cannot be encompassed by the little boy, but will be received, recorded, and jettisoned off into unconscious outer space. This child, who does not know what he knows, may tremble in the presence of certain stimuli. The fear or anxiety he feels in various situations will make no sense to him. He may think something is wrong with him. His emotions have not forgotten what he knows. Suddenly or gradually, through repeated exposure to similar fragments of the original event, the child will have the opportunity to retrieve his consciousness. If as he grows he develops skill with emotion, he will be somewhat prepared to manage himself during the return of the meteor of consciousness. The retrieval of consciousness happens through flashback. Details in the here and now trigger emotional response with enough frequency and/ or intensity to produce a "video," in whole or in part, of the original event. The experience is not solely visual but also extremely sensual and emotional. The largeness of the room, the coldness of the floor, the smells in the air, the quiet amid the violence—the trauma returns with the ferocity of the original experience.

Living with pieces of consciousness and psychic energy split off through dissociation or denial is like seeing with one eye. It can be done, functional adjustments are made, but full function is impaired. Emotional memory is a powerful resource. All the data necessary for full functioning is held there, waiting for the need and the willingness to use it.

Dependability of emotional memory

Since it records all the details of all of our experiences, emotional memory can provide information for review and reassessment. Emotional memory supports conscious, verbal functioning. It is that place which we access and dig around in to remember what we know. Not only is this way of knowing the first way an infant knows, it is the primary way information is received throughout life. In school, if a student receives information only through his verbal channels, he will have to repeat the entry frequently to store the information in brain memory. If the teacher can give the student an experience around the new information, then the student's emotional system participates in the learning. The story the teacher told, or whatever way the teacher had of bringing the information to life, has greater likelihood of being remembered than the verbal entry. This emotional, experiential means of knowing is dependable.

My conscious awareness of this way of knowing began only fifteen years ago. I was a new graduate student, having returned to school after eleven years at home raising four children. I was excited and challenged as I used my mind (or so I thought) in this way again. I was working through the family therapy courses and was growing familiar with the women and men whose work has been foundational to systemic thinking. Carl Whitaker is one of those persons. Dr. Whitaker's thinking and experience as a therapist have been tremendously generative in, as well as foundational to, the field of family therapy. Well, Carl Whitaker was in Toledo for a two-day seminar. I was positioned in the front row, pencils and paper ready. I wanted to record everything I possibly could of this opportunity. The seminar began and so did I, recording phrases, concepts, history, etc. I was writing as fast as I could, almost every word—even the word "Whoa!" When no more words followed "Whoa," I looked up to find Dr. Whitaker looking down at me. I scrambled to put "Whoa" into context; my face flushed red. Dr. Whitaker invited me to put my pencil down: "Everything I'm going to say is not so important." I was having an experience, and it was my emotional memory recording now. "Anyway, whatever you need to find out will go inside and it will cook," he said. Cook?! What does "cook" mean or have to do with anything? I put my pencil down and began to learn how information is really received. It was difficult for me. My well-trained verbal skills kept wanting to take off with that pencil. My distrust birthed fear that I was missing this opportunity. But my emotional memory went right on capturing the entire event immensely more completely than my pencil could. This felt like a shift into foreign territory, for I was not yet familiar with the amazing, steady, trustworthy data base that has always been there. Thank you, Carl Whitaker. Understanding that I "cook" has allowed me much peace and empowerment.

How emotional experience shapes principles and beliefs

Early experiences and the emotional learning which results create the program according to which we function. The process is not unlike the effect of DNA molecules, which determine pigmentation, growth patterns, and other physical characteristics at the moment of conception. Early emotional experience determines values, pursuits, needs, coping skills, and a great deal more. Much of the program is in place before we are verbal. It is a process as amazing and powerful as genetics, but unlike genetics, the emotional programming can be amended and extended.

After putting a Rubik's Cube in order or puzzling something out, one may not be able to say how the solution was reached. However, the process of the figuring can be taken apart and the steps of the process discerned. As the steps are discerned, they can be verbalized. Verbally encoding, or giving words to what we know, allows the information to become conscious and useable. Frequently, a question on a test may require that a student put several pieces of information together and reach a conclusion she has not yet reached. The principles of the conclusion reside within her and have not yet, until she tackles the question, been verbally encoded. It is a useful test that allows that kind of stretch. Similarly, emotional experiences mix in our core. Our principles and beliefs form from those experiences. Those principles and beliefs are the foundation of the programming that determines how we function. Many of the principles and beliefs are not verbally encoded. Many of our emotional experiences occur before we are verbal or capable of abstract thought. This essential information is available to us, but some life test must ask the question which propels our search that results in its verbalization.

The young man I spoke of in chapter one who is dedicated to not being affected by his dad's drinking works himself to the point of exhaustion, irritability, and physical illness in his efforts to be a good provider. When he is leaving for work, even though he is too sick or irritated to go, the question "Why are you going when you feel so awful?" could initiate a search. The young man may respond with concrete words about bills to be paid. Pursuing the question could open the opportunity to identify what he has not put into words before: "Because I can't let down like my dad did." As life events ask us to verbally encode our emotional learning, we begin to have access to the information it contains. It is then we can actively use our own program, instead of being driven by it. The young provider can have the chance to see that he has not let down and that taking care of himself is an important part of not being like his father.

The hologram

I have this idea that while we are handling the tangible elements of our daily lives, we bump into things that don't exist today and can no longer be touched. These things that have no substance today can be felt and even seen. If this sounds magical, I think it is. In the spaces where there aren't chairs, buildings, trees, cars, or people, there are the echoes of every day before this one. What amazing encounters are possible, as parts of today trigger feelings which wrap around the echoes and combine with the sound waves to create something to bump into. The bumping allows this something to be felt, not tactilely, since it has no substance, but emotionally. Just a little bit of one's curiosity can produce a vision: First, the emotional bump, then "Oh, what was that?" followed by a little silence and sensual tuning, and a colorful, talking motion picture may appear in the spaces where there is nothing. A hologram. A picture that doesn't require a camera. A picture projected between you and what is "real" or tangible.

There is a ride at Disney World where holograms dance and sing and speak in the spaces; they are ghosts of some other time and place in a fantastic ride created for the enjoyment of anyone who will come aboard. In the *Star Wars* trilogy, Luke Skywalker discovered the same kind of picture. Through it, he encountered his sister for the first time and made some important decisions and commitments.

One evening in early summer about two years ago, I was riding my bike, savoring the sounds of the day as it was about to end. Kids were enjoying more play before being called in, and some adults were out taking time to visit. The birds were making their evening noises. It was peaceful and pleasant. A man was putting his lawnmower away, and as I rode by his yard, the smell of freshly cut grass transported me to a different street, in a time long since past. I rode through the curtain of a time warp, and on the other side I was ten years old, riding down the street where I grew up. The sounds and smells of the present day created a vivid picture of an earlier day. I remembered neighbors I hadn't thought of for a long time. I was aware of perspective and detail: their houses in relation to mine, how the neighbors were in their yards, the black-and-white Oldsmobile that one of them drove. I was revisiting. It was powerful and wonderful. I had a sense of how I fit into that neighborhood. I could sense my smallness in it and my feeling of belonging to it. I reexperienced my affection for the older neighbors and how I liked to visit with and listen to them. I felt the comfort of that again. That bike ride was a spectacular experience.

I think we have countless opportunities for similar "rides" or experiences. The price of admission is only the willingness to feel a bit. Each ride brings more of our story to life. We may come to know it as well as the words to a favorite song or the plot of a touching film. Our own story can come to life and inspire, motivate, and empower us.

Feelings and fingertips: an analogy

Have we been told so often that we "shouldn't feel that way" or learned that emotion should occupy so little of life that feeling becomes unfamiliar business? I like to make an analogy between feelings and fingertips. Nerve endings in fingertips receive information and communicate with the brain. A very nice helpful flow goes back and forth. Fingertips sense something of high intensity, and the brain works with the nerve endings. The experience gets named: "hot." Expression and action follow in rapid succession. "Ouch!" Fingertips move. This process is neat, efficient, very useful.

"Hot" is one feeling I helped our kids with. I made sure they knew all the objects in their environment that fit into that category. When they were very little, I would say the word with feeling, and my face would show apprehension and caution. Each little person in his or her own time would repeat "hot!"

with feeling and understanding. I showed them how to respect hot things and what to do if they were hurt by heat. I told them about times I was burned and what I did. They saw me get burned by the oven, and they witnessed my expression and how I helped myself.

I think feelings have the same purpose as nerve endings in fingertips. Feelings can discern danger and safety so we know whether to stop or continue. Feelings can make needs apparent and can guide actions to satisfying creative choices. Feelings can make one's own behavior and the behavior of others intelligible. Feelings help me to keep myself separate from you, and feelings allow me to experience tremendous valuing and intimacy with others. Essential stuff.

"Stuffing feelings in our socks"

We have the opportunity in this culture to develop very few skills with feelings, except to "stuff them in our socks." That wonderful image belongs to George, and he has allowed me to borrow it. The image was born, I think, as George began to look for his feelings. Perhaps by stuffing feelings in our socks, we hope that walking on them will sufficiently extinguish them. It doesn't happen like that, however. The feelings make their way back up through our body where they were originally experienced, and there they lie and wait for expression and release. Feelings don't wait passively, however. Feelings seek every similar opportunity that occurs in the present to get up and out.

They reverberate through the body, rising to the surface in anticipation of the door opening. If no expression is allowed, the feelings will knock on the viscera and deep body tissue, demanding expression. If still denied, the insistence of feelings may increase blood pressure, cause burning in the stomach, or produce palpitation in the heart. The body may have to clamp down hard and long to contain the feelings. Headaches, muscle knots, worn teeth and jaw muscles, and bent bodies may result. Eventually some compulsion may be enlisted to aid in the fight against feelings. Alcohol anesthetizes, high carbohydrate foods soothe anxiety, long hours of work distract, vomiting and orgasm provide some catharsis.

Why continue with such great effort and devastating physical consequence? There is tremendous instruction from familial and societal culture that prohibits expression of feelings. Unfortunately, it is the repression of feelings that results in the outcomes that scare society and family.

A young mom's experience

Beginning to develop skills with feelings is an awkward, vulnerable experience, one that evokes a sense of incompetence. When I was a young mom, I felt competent if I didn't know I was anxious, overwhelmed, or sad. That was an important time to feel competent, but it was also an important time to feel whatever was there to be felt. I could have learned to develop real competence, instead of getting good at convincing myself I was competent. And that would have make a difference for our kids too.

There were so many feelings cooking in me in those early years of marriage and mothering. Unfortunately and unintentionally, my kids became responsible for the feelings I was stuffing. Instead of having the opportunity to hear their mother speak clearly about what she was feeling and to learn from her skills with feelings, my kids, in various and unique ways, began to sense my feelings and make meanings about them. Often the meanings were about themselves. If I was frustrated, tired, or overwhelmed, my feelings got connected with their behavior: they either did something wrong or should act to do something right to save me from my feeling. The clarity and distinction between us got lost. I was not taking time to feel me, and they lost themselves by taking over my job; they were busy sensing me since I wasn't sensing myself. This created mush and enmeshment. Some of that stickiness is still around today. We recognize it when we get caught in it. Our eyes exchange knowing glances and we work to peel ourselves away from it. We've gotten pretty good at the peeling, and the results are wonderful. We each get our distinctness back, and then there can be real intimacy again. That is very, very nice.

Erin's story

When kids sound like little adults, perhaps we need to listen to their wisdom. One day while in some feeling state, I was going on and on with my then nine-year-old daughter, Erin, about some of her behavior. She listened for awhile and then in a clear, firm voice said, "Mother, you are projecting your feelings on me." Her words were like a bolt of lightning. Exactly! It was so clear I couldn't deny it. How could a nine-year-old know this? Where did she get the words? It was the dawning of my awareness. How I wish all of my behavior could have changed with that first awareness. This is some of the stickiness that Erin and I still work at today. Thank you, Erin, for keeping your sense of yourself and having the courage to ask me to take responsibility for myself. That's a fantastic lesson for a nine-year-old to teach her mom. This was one of those times I began to realize that our family would change and grow from the bottom up as well as the top down. Realizing that, and making room in the family for it to happen, honors the children and empowers both the children and the adults.

Casey's story

Casey was an easy, gentle child. If I said "no," he didn't. He shared everything he had with his little brother, who arrived fifteen months into Casey's childhood. Casey had one temper tantrum over that; he ended it face down, crying a heartbroken cry on the kitchen floor. He learned to make clever noises to get our attention when he needed it, but he also learned to be too patient with the busy pulse of our family life. Finally, I realized how little he asked of us. Casey was getting little time and little touching. At first, Casey resisted my efforts to reconnect with him. He would turn and stretch his arm out when I bent to cuddle him in his bed. I would ask him questions and he would pretend not to hear or he would move away to play with his toys. Casey taught me to be persistent in my commitment to reconnect with him. We did it together, very slowly, as Casey's trust built. At first I'd ask Casey if he would hug me and count to ten. He would count fast. After awhile I would ask for a twenty count. When he wanted to tell me something, I would stop what I was doing so I could listen to and look at him. I was very grateful that this dear little child was willing to take his chances with me again. Casey is now a massive, six-foot young man who gives the warmest hugs and shares much with us.

Charlie's story

One cold, sunny winter's day, three-year-old Charlie and I took four-year-old Casey to nursery school. Casey was going sledding with his class and his eyes were wide and eager in anticipation. It was a great day for sledding and there was much excitement among the nursery classmates, who were stuffed into snow suits and walking like little penguins. After leaving Casey with his group, Charlie and I were walking back to the car. I heard some disgruntled muttering coming from the little penguin whose hand I was holding. I reached down and picked him up. "What did you say?" I asked. "I hate sledding!" was the reply from the mad-looking little mouth. For some reason unknown to me, I did not tell him how much fun sledding is, nor that he would be able to go when he was old enough for nursery school. I did not even tell him that we could go sledding soon, and he'd see how much fun it is. From somewhere beyond myself, I was able to do a very simple thing: I heard him. "You wish you could go sledding?" The mad around his mouth collapsed, and Charlie laid his head on my shoulder as we returned to the car together. No fixing, no making the feeling go away, just hearing. We were both close and safe.

Transcendent moments

The moments I have just described with Erin, Casey, and Charlie are precious to me. Precious mostly because I took the opportunity to savor the beauty and presence of their beings. Precious also because they were beginning moments for me. They were initiations into what is really going on. Those moments are, for me, spiritual. Ordinary experience was transformed by the communication of one spirit to another. Moments of transcendence, of not getting stuck in black-and-white, he said-she said, right-or-wrong control turbulence. Interactions like these with each of our children over the years have challenged me and instructed me. It is one of the awesome things about family experience; so much of the learning goes from the child to the parent. The way I look at it, their persons have demanded that I respect them and hear them. They have helped me get my verbal, scientific, linear thinking out of the way, and I have been able to return with them to the way of knowing that we are born with.

Experiencing holograms of the past

I think that if we believe in feelings, we get to take the ride, the ride that lets us bump into things that are no longer there and lets us experience all that went before in the presence of all that followed since. The ride reveals holograms of our own story. I believe that if we trust feelings, we will be able to stand the sensations that arise in our bodies as we bump into the past through some bit of the present. The sensations may be strong and confusing since nothing is there: "There's no reason for me to feel this way." But if we believe in and value emotions, we can get curious in spite of the intensity and confusion.

Getting curious is very different from getting angry at or embarrassed by the trance that begins to take place: "This is stupid!" or "Why am I feeling this way?" Getting curious sounds like: "What a strange thing to feel now, which is not the best time since I have to go start a meeting or when we are all about to have fun. I wonder what it is?" When a significant person or object or some similarity between yesterday and today evokes a feeling, curiosity will allow a hologram to appear. The feeling may rumble like an earthquake or come up like a little burp. Questions like "What is this like?" or "When did I feel like this before?" help get the hologram up for viewing. A dialogue can develop, either between you and the person you were in the hologram, or between the you that asks the questions and the you that begins to dig around in the emotional memory for the answer. As in any dialogue, communication is two-way; the learning can be also. As "all that followed since" listens to "all that went before," marvelous pieces of early programming get verbalized, encoded, and therefore available. When this has happened to me, my response has been, "No kidding, that's amazing!"

A personal example

One night at the office, I had just finished a family session and was about to begin a group therapy session, when I checked the messages on the answering machine. I heard my sister's voice telling me that she and my brothers were going to meet at my dad's house at 7:30 to go through his clothes and personal possessions. My father had recently died and, since he was our last parent, we had to inventory all the items in his home for his estate. We had been meeting regularly each week to do this, room by room. This meeting I was just hearing about had not been previously scheduled, and it was beginning at the same time my group was. I couldn't get to my dad's house until close to 9:30. I began to tremble. A very inconvenient time to tremble. I had notes to make regarding the family session and pressing physical needs to take care of. I needed to switch gears to be ready and available for the group session. The trembling didn't care. It didn't stop; it was very insistent. I had to ask what this was, writing as I asked the questions. I saw and felt a little near-sighted girl on the fringe of a crowd of bigger people, most of them family. In the next image I saw, she was sitting alone on the back steps of a cottage we used to rent, sitting alone while everyone else was gathered inside. It was a curious picture, different from my previous memories of the cottage. I really wanted to know what this was about. It was as if I was in a dialogue with the little girl on the back steps. I asked what she was feeling. She felt like something terrible was going to happen. I didn't like the feeling I was having. It didn't make sense and I wanted it to go away. I tried soothing it, assuring myself that nothing terrible would happen. Then I realized that making the feeling go away would only have buried it again. What terrible thing was going to happen? The little girl didn't know; she only knew how it felt.

Well, how did it feel? The trembling and urgency in the pit of my stomach helped to name the feeling: "Like I won't exist." If my head had not been out of the way of this whole experience, it might have said, "That's crazy!" But in an instant, so much made sense. As a child, I had gotten lost at family gatherings. All that was going on and all the commotion had a life without me. My nearsightedness must have added to the lostness. The probably often-repeated experience had left a belief deep inside me that I had no idea was there: "You don't matter!" As soon as I verbalized and encoded the feeling, two things happened. First a calm began to spread over me. Then, instinctively, my hands went to my lap and held on right above my knees. Communication had come from the little girl in the hologram to me when I learned that there was a belief inside me that had long needed changing. And then communication went spontaneously from me back to those early emotional experiences when my hands held on, as if to say: "You do exist, and matter." Another part of my story had become available to me.

I was able to go on to and be available for my group. I very much wanted to be with my siblings as they approached my dad's belongings. I was missing something very important, but I wasn't going to cease to exist. That was a relief. I was able to accept the position I was in. I had a sense now of how difficult it must have been for my sister Lynne, who lives eight hours away and couldn't be with us for those important events.

Changing emotional beliefs

The concepts of emotional memory and holograms allow

some things to happen that never had a chance to happen before. Feelings can get out—feelings that had no words then and no one to go to. As feelings begin to come out, there are many opportunities to feel incompetent and to struggle with these new emotional experiences. When we take these opportunties to struggle, we develop skills with emotions. The first skill is making the room to do it. Stumbling around to find the words to express what has not been verbalized before is the second skill. Finding names for the feelings is another. Expressing and naming contribute to development of an additional skill—how to respond to the feeling. That's the action part, like moving your fingers when you touch something hot. As we use and develop these simple skills, we hook up again to our gut knowing. That's power, baby! All systems are go. So much is possible now. Not only does the stuff come out and learning take place, but also missing pieces can be filled in and information that was inadvertently left out can be supplied. Emotional beliefs and meanings made can be amended or removed.

Repeated emotional experience, not intellectualization, changes emotional beliefs. If we learned that we are responsible for someone's feelings, we did so through emotionally intense experience. The intellectual realization that we are not responsible for another's feelings has little impact on relinquishing that responsibility. Repeating "I am not responsible," "I am not responsible" while trying to give up responsibility is not a very effective intervention. Taking the opportunity to emotionally and experientially let learning enter begins to produce real change. Because the original beliefs entered the data base through repeated emotional experiences, it takes more than one emotional experience to reprogram a belief. But even one such experience has a profound effect. In that experience, we are able to bring together what we know now with what we believed then, and the latter experience is forever changed.

Using the stuff that bubbles up from early emotional experience empowers. Missing pieces can be filled in. Emotional beliefs and meanings can be amended or removed.

I remember when I had the opportunity to return to my paternal grandmother's home thirty-some years after her death. I had stayed with her as a very small child on our trips to Pittsburgh. I remembered the pattern on her kitchen floor. I had a sense of watching her move about her very large kitchen, fixing me breakfast, and I recalled the grand dining room she would serve me in. When I revisited that space, I was astonished to find both rooms very small. This new experience collided with my childhood experience, and much like the way a word processor incorporates new words and rear-ranges a document, my early experience got rearranged. My smallness had made the room so big, and my grandmother's special presence had enlarged the experience for me. I can still sense all that, but I have updated my awareness also.

Doing your own work

I believe that life constantly gives us opportunities for these updating experiences. These experiences allow us to finish our own self-work so we don't have to keep trying to hoodwink someone else into doing it. They also allow us to heal ourselves so we don't have to find a magic person to do that for us. So much useless, painful effort goes into the pursuit of Good Parent and Magic Healer. Lives are led down tangled, heartbreaking trails. Years can be spent trying to force a lover to respond the way a child of long ago needed a parent to respond. Years of an-ger and frustration pass as lovers try to arm wrestle each other into positions that fill their own needs.

These attempts are the undoing of the relationship and of the partners themselves. Persons who began an adult-to-adult rela-tionship get entranced and transfer to their partners the feelings and expectations a child would have for a parent. The fact that it happens is not the problem; such transference will take place. Not recognizing when it happens is the problem.

The Good Parent trance can also create pain in the relationship between parents and their children. It is common for parents to want to give their children all that they did not have in their own childhood. Instead of providing those missing pieces for themselves, parents try to supply their children with what they missed. The child ends up being coerced into accepting what her parents needed. It is a mystery to the child. She may recognize her parents' need to give, and so will patiently accept. But she may see their giving as a message about herself. For instance, a child given all the guidance and protection her parent once needed may begin to think that the parent does not trust her or believe she can take care of some things for herself. I have seen young people severely depressed or greatly angry in reaction to this struggle. Parents may be dismayed by their child's seeming lack of gratitude for having everything that the parents lacked. I have seen parents feel used, ignored, and unvalued as a result.

The search for Magic Healer is devastating too. In the pursuit of our own healing, we may seek to give healing or to receive it. Those "looking for" manage to hook up with those "giving," and such a dance they do! If the hookup is successful, an insatiable cycle results. The medicine man or woman is healing or rescuing a child who will always need the medicine person's magic. The healer is looking for the satisfaction of having supplied the right medicine. The relationship, having been negotiated on the basis of wounded and healer, revolves in this never ending cycle. Even the most willing healer loses patience or becomes bored or disgusted by the ever present neediness. The wounded get it again: more rejection, more abandonment.

A child's eyes rightfully look to the adult for protection, comfort, and guidance. That works for relationships between children and adults. I don't believe that it works in adult-to-adult relationships. The work of healing, finishing, and remaking emotional beliefs belongs to one's self. This needs to be self-work, because the self needs to possess the results. When one is dying, there is no question as to who is doing the work. Friends, family, and lovers can support and enhance that experience, but only the dying one can do it. That's how I think it is with finishing and healing. After each person accepts the responsibility for this work and initiates it, the need-meeting and enhancement that takes place in relationships is safe and satisfying. Undertaking the self-work involves gaining access to the emotional memory. The notion of the hologram is one way of conceptualizing and visualizing past emotional residue, in order to render it useable.

Using the stuff that bubbles up from early emotional experience empowers. The empowerment happens as more of self becomes available to self. The unconscious does not have to remain a strange, mysterious part of ourselves. It's the part where all experience is recorded. It has great power in our lives. We can break into the control room of the unconscious and harness the energy source. Doing so means being able to ride the horse instead of being dragged by it. Taking that responsibility on allows so much to be possible in relationships, in work, and in the fantastic experience of living.

Chapter five

Relatedness Within: Developing Integrity, Using Conflict, Experiencing the "Perfect Ordeal"

The echoes of previous emotional experiences are powerful and persistent. They arise out of the noise produced in the world around us. The echoes come unsolicited and they flood our senses. Certain songs, the sun after a series of gray Midwest days, the smell of freshly cut grass or leaves burning, hands that look like someone's who loved you, joy or pain on a child's face, a funeral cortege, someone's anger, the way an old man walks, the feelings a frown imparts, a touch, or the void that the absence of it leaves—brief moments that punctuate each day's experience. These can all be dismissed as a nostalgic moment, a distraction, a wandering mind, or an annoying interference, each dismissal implying that the echoes turn one away from what is really important. But the echoes are persistent, returning again and again to defy the dismissal. Our willingness to notice the echo and then to allow its resonance to stir and beckon creates the opportunity to develop integrity. Each echo invites the end of the segregation of emotional knowing from verbal knowing. As we learn to coordinate these two powerful resources, an internal unity develops. Integrity is the result. Integrity is defined as soundness, the state of being undivided, an unimpaired condition. That sounds good. And it feels good.

Such integrity develops through repeated access to and use of emotional memory. With this integrity, the full range of experience opens and becomes available to us. If the dominant hand is like verbal/rational knowing, the nondominant hand can be analogous to emotional knowing. The nondominant hand is not employed as frequently and, therefore, is not as facile. It lies dormant while we write, draw, cut, list, or figure, supplying a supportive service from time to time. In some pursuits, both hands perform equally: typing, playing the piano, sweeping, buttoning. It's hard to imagine doing any of those things without both hands, though with effort and improvisation, they can be done. What is lost in playing the piano with one hand is like what is lost in life experience by allowing verbal/rational knowing to function alone without emotional knowing. The dormant hand longs to be used, to perform and participate.

In the orchestration of everyday life, emotional memory keeps sending out a reprise. Themes and strains and fragments repeat. The echoes beckon. "Let the memory live again!" The invitation is haunting and persistent. Like the song "Memory" from the musical *Cats*, it begs, "Touch me! It's so easy to leave me...!" It promises, "If you touch me, you'll understand what happiness is." The song "Memory" speaks of transformation, of a new life. Learning to become powerful with both "hands," developing coordination and complementarity between rational and emotional knowing, produces the transformation. Becoming more abled is what the transformation is about. Having use of only one hand would be considered a disability. Recovering function adds ability. The integrity that results from the coordination of verbal and emotional knowing adds tremendous ability. Awareness of what is going on in any situation is far greater when the data feeding the awareness comes from both sources. Life lived taking in information from only or mainly the verbal/cognitive source is flat and one-dimensional, compared to the rich awareness available from the coordination of both. Every observation and perception becomes enhanced. It is the difference between black and white or color, one dimension or many. We become infinitely more capable of fully appreciating what is going on in everyday events and encounters.

Many daily events slip by without demanding much attention or awareness. It is those moments in relationships where our differences come upon each other that stress us to become more aware. Differences are startling. The surprise and stress may be unsettling. We encounter each other, and differences may seem to threaten closeness. But when our differences threaten to set us apart, they also provide the opportunity for intimacy. To approach that intimacy, we must be able to understand the usefulness of conflict.

Conflict as an aid to growth and intimacy

Conflict is defined as the act of striking together. Perhaps much like a whetstone sharpens the knife that strikes against it, persons in relationship are whetstones for each other, each becoming more distinct by the act of striking together. Some of the striking may be playful, as when the distinctness of each person's sense of humor banters with the other. It's a kind of jousting that is enjoyable and can be full of energy. In the interaction, each person holds his/her own, and the differences cause a delightful interplay. Differences can create tenderness when one reaches out in affection, caressing and valuing the other. The striking together is passionate when the interplay becomes sexual. And the striking together is dif-

> *Life lived taking in information from only the verbal/rational source is flat and one-dimensional, compared to the rich awareness available by including emotional knowing.*

ficult when differences between persons cause challenge and confusion. This painful kind of conflict is every bit as useful and important in a relationship as the other kinds of striking together. In fact, this conflict is essential to self-development and growth and intimacy.

We live in a society where conflict is assumed to be negative. Conflict designates war. And conflict in a relationship is deemed to mean trouble. Often conflict is taken as a sign the relationship is fundamentally flawed. But conflict is as essential as beating hearts and breathing.

I like to think of conflict on a continuum. On one end is the striking together that occurs as parent holds infant, the bumping together of who the baby is with who she isn't. She is being loved, valued, and supported by who she isn't, and a space is made for her to become all she can be. The conflict between parents and adolescents is on the same end of the continuum. The young person must push the limits, and parents must learn when to yield and when to hold firm; then both can exist and grow together. Lovers, friends, siblings, coworkers are bound to experience conflict as they live or work together. As much as it is inevitable, it is also essential. The challenge of the conflict creates room for the differences between persons, and it also demands that each person stretch and grow. Conflict in all its forms is the beating heart of the relationship. It means there is life and action in the relationship. The conflict pushes each person to be more himself/herself while demanding continued growth. Conflict creates distinctness and sharpness as the two persons strike together. It makes room for each so that a "we" can exist without loss of either "I."

On the other end of the conflict continuum is the reactive stuff. That is where the wars are. It is what happens if people don't make some sense and use of the challenge of conflict. Unfortunately, this reactive extreme is where much of our experience with conflict resides. Our understanding of conflict and our attempts to resolve conflict come from our experience in this reactive extreme.

Another definition of conflict is "the opposition of persons or forces that gives rise to dramatic action...." I like that. Such dramatic action it is! In order to appreciate the drama, it is necessary to understand the importance and usefulness of the opposition and the inevitability of it as well. The differences between persons give rise to the conflict. Often much effort is put into dissolving differences. Usually each side of an opposition knows what the other should do in order to avoid the conflict. I want you to change behavior so as not to cause the disruption. I can see what you should do differently in order to avoid the disruption. If you would just control your temper and be grateful for what you have in life... Meanwhile you may be thinking how the upset could be avoided if I weren't so critical and pushy... The underlying assumption is: you should be more like me or more how I want you to be. That's just a little arrogant. More troubling than that narrow, egocentric view is the sameness we often want the differences to dissolve into. The desire for everyone in the family to be the same is the energy that pushes for enmeshment. No difference, no conflict—everyone operating according to someone's view of how it should be. The cost is loss of difference, loss of self, loss of a dynamic process. And loss of any hope for intimacy. Fortunately, differences don't vanish, so the opportunities for conflict return.

The action of oppositions often originates at very inconvenient times. It is challenging and confusing. It is usually upsetting. So it's understandable why one would want to make it go away completely. But it is here to stay because it is inherent in the differences between persons. And it has a purpose.

The "perfect ordeal"

The dramatic action created by an opposition brings up for each side some of the most powerful and deepest emotional experiences and beliefs. It makes a significant relationship a living drama. I believe a marriage is "made in heaven" when I see the husband's behavior and ways triggering the deepest emotional experience of his wife, and vice-versa. I think we choose our mates with the unconscious part of ourselves; our guts do the choosing. Our visceral, emotional part recognizes some things that cannot be spoken because they are not yet encoded and conscious. Our guts find the person who will create the "perfect ordeal." In marriage we sign up to go on each other's odyssey. The marriage contract takes us to the depth of each other's being, to swim around in the pain and confusion as well as the joy and sweetness there. In marriage, I wed my self to your stuff and you to mine.

I may want to move differently than you do in a three-legged race, and we'll laugh at the struggle we have getting to the finish line. We may not be laughing over the conflict produced by the union of my stuff and your stuff. We'll cry and wonder if we were mad in making the choice to unite. Some days we'll shake right down through our guts to our bones. If we can hang on and puzzle it out, what unfolding and intimacy are in store. The "perfect ordeal" creates a trip unlike any other. We travel to the distant reaches of each other's being, unraveling mysteries all the way. We swim, at times, in the center of each other's life, and with each visit we learn more about what Life Itself knows of living, its origin, its meaning, and its destination. All the years of the travel and conflict force us against each other and wear us to such distinction that we can tolerate an incredible amount of intimacy just because we are so aware of our own selves. That self-awareness comes through uncovering each inch of the boundary of our own selfhood. Because of the power of the "perfect ordeal," those are inches one doesn't forget.

The ordeal. Every person who has ever been in a relationship has experienced it. Encountering the ordeal feels terrible, often devastating. The experience of that encounter belies the wonderful invitation the ordeal extends. Often the ordeal involves "trivial" things.

Alice and Bob's story: recognizing the ordeal

After work one day, Alice hurried home to get some things done before an evening meeting. She started some laundry and made a quick-though-respectable dinner. It was a satisfying feeling for Alice; she had good food ready for Bob and the kids, the table looked inviting, and all that went into the meal preparation was cleaned up and put away. Her family could come to the table, enjoy each other and the food she prepared, and have very little to do afterward. Alice would go on to her meeting knowing her family would experience her caring even though she would not be present. The meeting dragged on, and Alice was very tired when she walked in the door at 10:15. She stepped past the jackets and the gym clothes on the back hall floor. "The kids can get that stuff in the morning," she thought. She hung her coat up, put her briefcase down, and turned on the kitchen light. As she heard the snap of the light switch, she felt something snap within her. Dinner dishes were scattered over the countertops; cereal boxes and sticky ice cream splashes detailed her family's evening activities. She found Bob and the kids cuddled together on the couch, having fallen asleep there while watching

TV. The snap inside Alice turned on outrage. "What have they done all evening?! The kids should have been in bed long ago. Why did they leave all this for me!?" Bob saw the look in her eye as soon as he woke. He hustled the kids to bed while Alice stomped around the house cleaning up. She was very angry when Bob met her in the kitchen. All her frustration and anger were pouring out. Bob was angry now, too. She had no idea what he had dealt with during the evening, and now he had her anger to deal with also. "What's important here?" he thought, "the people or the countertops!?"

This wasn't the first time this particular conflict surfaced between them, and it wouldn't be the last. Each person was tired and disgusted. Bob wanted to get it over with, go to bed, and start a new day. Alice didn't want to let it go; she wanted Bob to realize so it would not happen again. Late in a long day the chances of being able to resolve the situation were slim. The chances of escalation were great. The moment Alice and Bob met in the kitchen was the peak of the ordeal; it was also the moment of invitation. Who needs an invitation like this? Heck of a time.

The invitation cannot be completely ignored because this ordeal will repeat. If Alice and Bob can hang onto the idea that they love and value each other—the *idea* of it because the feelings of love and valuing are far away at this moment—they have a chance. If they also can know that very important things

are embedded in all of this, they have an even better chance—
the chance to not give up on each other. They can do what they
need to do for themselves to end the day, and they can make
time with each other to work this out.

Without the participants having some very specialized skills,
an ordeal can only escalate once it has begun. The reactive cycle
will play out, and the partners will be spent at the end, hopeless
and believing they are enemies. What to do before the skills are
developed is to stop. But in order to stop, they must be able to
appreciate the invitation the ordeal offers. That simply means
being able to acknowledge that some very important issues for
each partner are embedded in this situation. It is the realization
that "something big is going on here." It is easy to know that
something big is going on because it feels big to each person.

There is temptation to trivialize what's going on, however.
"Men are like that!" "She must be premenstrual." But it is the
persons who get trivialized. There is temptation to avoid the invitation by letting it blow over or by bringing flowers, or to finish it by punishing with silence or withdrawal. Partners get skillful then at demeaning, avoiding, apologizing, and punishing.

The acknowledgement that "something very powerful is
happening here" allows the couple to stop the escalation and accept the invitation. In this powerful interplay between Bob and
Alice, the escalation will stop if they can acknowledge that a lot
is going on that they don't yet understand. They will keep faith

with each other by stopping the escalation and by admitting that they want to understand but 11 o'clock at night may not be the time. Each can find a way to begin to unwind, knowing each has a partner who won't walk away from this.

The ordeal's three realities

In the ordeal between Alice and Bob there are three realities present at once. Not only is there the "here and now" reality of the collision in the kitchen; there is an "as if" reality for each partner. Within the present collision, each of them has also collided with a sizeable, emotion-rich hologram from the past. Alice feels "expendable" when she does all she does for her family, then comes home and finds still more to do. As a young girl at home, Alice had felt expendable. Her mom kept cleaning up after everyone, and Alice was expected to do the same as the oldest daughter. Bob feels "less important" than the things in the house. Bob's parents had been very poor as kids and had taught their children to take extraordinary care of things. The emphasis on taking care of things made the things seem more valuable than the people.

Attempting to resolve the "here and now" issues without reference to the other two realities is dangerous. It leads to "right-wrong," "did too!-did not!" escalation. Someone is wrong, crazy, or stupid. So much is going on that doesn't meet the eye. Very significant experiences and beliefs of each partner are embedded in the context of the "here and now" reality. If those get pushed aside, so too do the uniqueness and significance of each person. Then the de-escalation will be achieved by one partner "winning" and one partner "compromising." Such a win and compromise will cheat them both.

The "as if" realities tap into some long-standing pain for each partner. Feeling expendable is devastating to Alice. She feels it in this situation, and she had felt it many times before. Each experience with it amplifies the next. For Alice, expendable feels like "you don't matter too much." So it's irrelevant if she is tired or has other things to do; she is still the one to do the cleanup work. Just being the main cleanup person over time communicates unimportance. The final blow is not being able to get her husband to understand. In fact, unwittingly, Bob communicates directly to her pain when he says "this is trivial." Alice feels caught in a hopeless web with no way out.

Bob is angry about reexperiencing the importance of things over people. He wants to do battle with that idea. It is very painful that what he does is not good enough, and it is deeply discouraging. He opens his eyes from sleep and sees an angry woman that he cannot satisfy. Unwittingly, Alice is communicating directly to Bob's pain when she pours out her frustration. It is this deadlock of the long-standing pain of each partner that causes the escalation in the conflict.

Let's look at the invitation that Bob and Alice's ordeal extends. Alice steps through the door and collides with a myriad of things to be done. She collides also with that awful feeling of being expendable. She was already exhausted before these two collisions. The invitation for Alice is to learn how to say "I can't do all this. I don't want to do all this. Just because I am a woman, I don't have to do all this." She'll remember she didn't like the arbitrariness of it when she was growing up: Just because she was the oldest daughter...what about her sisters?...her brothers? She knew then that the work should be shared.

Bob awakens and sees the displeasure of an angry woman. He gets Alice mixed up with Mom. He has an important message for his wife, but he must get it first himself: "People are more important than things." Once he's sure of that, he won't get his wife mixed up with his mother, and he won't have to fight the same fight with her that he fought with his mom. He'll know that he and Alice are both more important than things, and he'll be able to work with her to keep it that way.

Reactive cycles escalate if we see only the "here and now" reality. Reactive cycles stop if each partner looks at his/her own "as if" reality. Intimacy results when the two share their realities with each other. And those very "as if" stories contain the elements of the resolution of the present dilemma.

So conflict happens. It always has. It always will. It is the nature of relationships. It has purpose. When there is conflict that hurts and is confusing, it's the ordeal playing out between two persons. After enough escalations, each side knows when it is time to stop. The acknowledgement of what will happen if they don't and the realization of what can happen if they do provide the impetus to stop. Then it's time for each person to turn to self and ask, "What is this for me?" and "How can I help myself right now?" Just that intervention produces awesome results. The war is stopped, and each person is learning and giving to self what is needed. Alice realizes she doesn't have to do it all. She learns that she needs to say when it's too much. Bob no longer fights the battle with his mom through his wife. He can accept what he knew as a child: people are more important. He doesn't need to let things go in order to prove it any more.

Sharing each "as if" reality

But there is more. After each person finds out about his or her own "as if" reality or trance, the trances can be shared. Each partner can draw his or her own picture for the other. It is possible to see the other side after stepping back and taking care of self. The sharing is like watching a film or play that portrays both stories. Each person can have empathy with the other. Bob learns how Alice feels expendable, and he comes to understand how discouraging that is for her. She learns what it's like for Bob to experience anger about things and how he begins to feel less important than things.

After working through this ordeal, Bob and Alice will be

able to do more with the next one. In addition to stopping the escalation and being able to help themselves, they will also be able to understand and care about what is happening for the other. It is a very special moment when, in the midst of your own strong emotion and awareness, you find great tenderness for the experience of your partner.

This is the experience of intimacy. It's this kind of intimacy that adds dimension to the physical sharing of bodies. When two people have stopped the war, taken responsibility for themselves, and been able to share each other's experience, sexual intimacy becomes the interplay between two spirits as well as two bodies. I don't think intimacy can be experienced without conflict. We certainly can get excited and passionate and can climax, and that's called physical intimacy. But it's over when it's over, not unlike eating a hot fudge sundae. You have to eat another one to get the feeling again. The spiritual intimacy that accumulates over a lifetime of learning what conflict has to teach is ever present. This spiritual intimacy enhances and transforms the sexual experiences that punctuate a relationship lived in responsiveness instead of reactiveness.

Responsiveness and relationship within

If any one thing can be said about a child, it is that a child is responsive. That responsiveness is a sign of life. The reflexes of a newborn are used to measure its healthfulness. In those first years, a child grows and accumulates knowledge by using all his/her senses. The child participates in life in a sensual, responsive way. What a delight to watch a baby enjoy her early experience with "solid" food—cereal, squash, etc. Her sense of smell and feelings of hunger have her alert and ready. She salivates before the food arrives, so it is ready to ooze out of her mouth before it gets in. The reflexive sucking action of her tongue helps to push half of it out, so she gets the thrill of sensing her food by touch too. Her hand comes to latch onto the spoon held by her dad. She is delighted, making noises as she approaches the food, eyes big in anticipation. Her hand and mouth lock onto the bite at the same moment. She touches the food that is dripping out of her mouth and squeezes it in her hand. Her body arches; she squeals and turns in her seat. All this over one bite, and it's all ready to happen again over the next. So alive, so ready to participate fully. This beautiful baby girl is a study in responsiveness! Every system of her body is grappling with this experience. And all the while she keeps contact with those around her.

We do need to develop social skills and not make such a mess while eating, but so much of our responsiveness gets lost as we grow. Babies and children provide reminders of how to use all our systems to receive and process information. As this little eating baby is learning about food and her relationship with her parents, she is developing coordination and complementarity between all her systems. She is developing relationship within herself. She is so open to it now. As she grows, she will be asked to sacrifice some of her relationship with herself for the sake of relationship with others. It will be a huge challenge to socialize, do what is expected, and not lose the tremendous presence she had.

It is this relationship within that produces self-esteem and is the dynamic process that develops and maintains the self. As a baby grows, the relatedness of all her systems grows and is refined. She is a masterpiece. So many systems—autonomic, neurochemical, central nervous, hormonal, emotional, intellectual, kinesthetic, etc.—are developing in harmony to empower an extremely capable human being. None of her internal relatedness needs to be sacrificed to be in relationships with others, or to go to school, or to work. Yet some of it will be. In fact, all of the relatedness within is essential in order to have rewarding relationships and work.

If we go back to watch that beautiful, eating baby girl again, we can see her unique characteristics developing. She will eat differently than her sister or her cousins did at that age, though there will be many similarities among the babies. All that a child takes in, as well as how she receives and processes the experiences that are provided and that happen, are the dynamic sources of her sense of self. She is unique from the start, unlike all the other babies as much as alike. As she grows, she will become like the members of her family, and she will also be very unlike them. If her unlikeness can be fostered as much as her likeness will be, she has a chance of keeping the wonderful presence she now has.

Fostering unlikeness

Unlikeness can feel threatening. Some of the ugliest actions humans are capable of have occurred in opposition to differences, both at the level of society and the family. In our efforts to impart values to our children, our expectations can become harnesses around their necks, unnecessarily so. The pressure we put on children to be like us and not scare us with their uniqueness is tremendous. In the process, we do great damage. We need to be able to tolerate unease and disharmony, to allow—even to foster—unlikeness. In encouraging the extraordinary specialness of the child, the family begins to have fresh options available, and the child has a chance to thrive.

Fostering unlikeness involves allowing a child as much choice as is appropriate and as we can stand. It means continuing to be amazed by and to celebrate the eccentric way the child expresses herself. Clamping down on the differences a child displays is a reaction to our own fear. And when our unease pushes us to fight and pressure for sameness, it is then that we create dis-ease. Learning how to tolerate the fright we feel in the presence of difference and to savor the uniqueness we see is at the heart of responsiveness to ourselves and our children.

Relatedness within

As human beings, we have tremendous capacities for feedback throughout all our systems. The feedback loops allow us to be responsive to ourselves. We shiver if cold, to generate warmth. If too much of a neurotransmitter piles up in a nerve synapse, the chemical systems adjust to produce less of that particular substance. After we sit in a certain position for a long time, our back muscles signal discomfort and we can make a conscious choice to change positions. If we lose our balance, our eyes can fix on a stationary object and equilibrium can be restored. If some system is chronically out of balance, a very loud signal may be sent out. The largeness of the signal may be devastating, as with a heart attack, but it does allow the opportunity for intervention. Without a physiological relatedness within, these magnificent feedback systems could not function.

Relatedness within encourages consciousness and increasingly higher levels of coordination of all the systems. Developing relatedness within is like slipping into the driver's seat on a vehicle that has a multitude of functions. The driver can learn to coordinate them all. And that takes ongoing development of skills; each level of coordination allows higher functioning that needs more skill development. The power of the driver keeps increasing. The sense of self and the empowerment of self keep growing.

This physiological internal relatedness, and the consciousness and responsiveness that evolve from it, are the elements that establish a relationship with self. Relationship with self is fundamental to all other relationships and to every pursuit of the self. The exhortation to love oneself implies the existence of relationship with self. When the focus of self is internalized, the result is the development of personal power and responsiveness to one's own needs and feelings. This internal power center is a place where messages from life experiences can be received and processed. The relationship with self creates the sanctuary where the human spirit can interface with the Eternal Spirit.

The reactive self

The largest impediment to the relationship with self is the disconnection of the emotional system from the other systems. The impediment is the lack of consciousness about the emotional system and all the information it can provide. Without connection to the emotional system, I don't believe that there can be a real self. Instead, there will be a reactive self that has developed in reaction to the needs, feelings, and expectations of others.

The reactive self is unstable and ungrounded; it is dependent upon the approval of others. The reactive self, lacking its own value in relationship within, must have another to be reacting to and taking readings from. Focus on the other motivates the action of the reactive self. Gestures and expressions, both verbal and behavioral, from the other are the evidence that the self is valuable or not valuable. It is a terrifying way to live. The reactive self cannot tolerate differences. The differences threaten precisely because they are not a validation of the self. The possibility of real relationship with others is relinquished. Instead, the other exists to be pleased, controlled, placated, or submitted to, as a means of deriving the sense of self-worth that sustains life.

The real self

Connection to the emotional system which develops increasing internal relatedness is the cornerstone of a real self. Inside are all the mechanisms that let us know how we are doing. Developing skill and responsiveness with feelings allows us to be quite aware of when we are being honest, if we are in trouble, if we do or say something abusive or unfair to another. When we are connected to our emotional system, we are able to know our own value and are able to hold onto that valuableness, even while realizing our shortcomings.

The real self has value independently of others, just like the infant or child does. The incredible presence and uniqueness of a baby or child are so captivating. It is abundantly clear that these radiant creatures have value just by virtue of their existence.

When emotional connection to self is lacking

To say that there cannot be a real self without conscious connection to the emotional system may sound like an overstatement. It may be comparable to stating that there can be no sound fiscal policy that does not involve responsible spending and establishment of a savings plan. Perhaps at this time those realities are so obviously lacking at the levels of government, institutions, and corporations, as well as at the personal level, that the need for them is urgent and therefore overvalued by virtue of that urgency. The need for connection and skill with the emotional system screams its urgency through the acts of violence, impulse, and compulsion that disturb us so as a society. The need and urgency highlight the importance of emotional relatedness with self.

Frequently I listen to persons tell about how angry they got, how depressed they've become, or how much they are consuming. I hear and understand their fear: "What is wrong with me?!!" One shouts obscenities at her mother, another puts a fist through the wall, one pounds on the chest of her partner, a dad strikes his daughter, one threatens self-annihilation, one drives a car into a ditch, another slowly starves himself. One eats huge amounts of food and vomits for catharsis; another consumes the food and keeps it. One works sixteen hours a day; another works all day and uses the money to buy a drug of choice. "What is wrong with me?!!" Many of those behaviors create a physiological consequence or reaction that causes habituation and addiction. Many of the behaviors initially or eventually occur because some emotional signal has been chronically unheeded. A cycle results: Unheeded needs and feelings provoke behavior which becomes compelling and dominant and which anesthetizes needs and feelings. Either the emotional feedback mechanism gets anesthetized or ignored or no response is made to the emotional signal due to lack of knowledge or skill. If early warning devices do not initiate response, some kind of emotional meltdown occurs. Then our behavior makes us look and feel crazy.

Broken cups: a personal story

When I was a little girl, probably about six years old, I did something that scared me. I remember it vividly still. My mother had a two-tiered end table, and on the bottom tier was a collection of small delicate cups and saucers. There was a little pink one with some white flowers sculpted around the cup and a very ornately painted one. I remember those two because I deliberately broke them. I remember being down in the basement with my mother, who was washing clothes. I don't know why I got so angry. When my father came down, I was sent upstairs. I have a sense of my fury. I remember seeing the cups and striking out at them. I don't know if the sense of their value and importance to my mother came to me before I struck out, but it certainly came after. I remember slumping over with my head in the seat of the chair next to the table. I was crying and looking at how irreversible the breaking was. I remember the feeling of knowing I had never seen my siblings do such a thing. It was awful; I must be awful! I remember being stuck between having done it and knowing my parents must find out I did it. I don't remember what happened next. My sense of how awful I was predominates.

Today I know that I was not crazy or awful. I must have had some tremendous feeling that I had no idea what to do with. Something important was going on with me, and I have no sense of what it was. I just remember the broken cups—the measure of my fury. When I struck out at my children as an angry, frustrated young mother, some of the same thing was going on. It's very important for a mother to know about her large feelings and develop skills with them so she doesn't strike out at children. I regret that striking out much more than the broken cups.

> *We choose our relationships with the unconscious part of ourselves; our guts find the persons who will create the "perfect ordeal."*

Relatedness with self, relationship with others

I think emotional volcanoes erupt if signals from the emotional system keep getting ignored, overruled, or anesthetized with compulsions. I find recovery of relatedness with self to be an essential and urgent priority.

It's a relief to realize that one isn't crazy, that rather some need, feeling, or unfinished business is screaming for attention. Emotional relatedness within self allows response before a need or feeling has to scream. Chronic patterns can be intervened on, and volcanoes and heart attacks can be averted. Energy goes to growth and development then, instead of to disaster cleanup.

Emotional availability is an exquisite presence of self that grows from the internal relationship. The presence is visible and palpable. When one is emotionally available, the human spirit is right behind the eyes and under the skin. The body is animated. Emotional availability with oneself creates the presence and skills necessary to establish and sustain relationship with others.

Learning to be responsive to one's own needs and feelings develops the skills of emotional responsiveness necessary in relationships with others, while making one a safe and trustworthy person to be with. The safety and trustworthiness mean that if my needs and feelings are known to me and dealt with by me, I am much less likely to be a volcano. If *my* spirit is safe with me, I am more likely to have the skills and awareness to be respectful of *your* spirit. The skills I develop in taking seriously the information from my emotional system allow me to be respectful of and more responsive to information from your emotional system.

Developing a relationship with self does not preclude relationships with others; it is foundational to them. Sometimes I find a fear in persons about developing relationships with themselves. They fear that by taking care of their own needs, they won't need anyone else. I believe that freedom from a certain basic level of neediness is exactly what makes relationship with another person possible to sustain. Partners are freed from parenting each other and can love and be close without losing themselves to or for the other. Wanting becomes the reason to be together instead of neediness.

Chapter six

The Self: Taking Responsibility, Coming Alive, Having Power

No one can do it for you. Getting a self is your job. People aren't being unloving or cruel when they refuse to do it for you. Not even a parent can give or make a self for a child. Parents can and ought to create conditions optimal for kids to develop their own selves. Parents have awesome responsibility and opportunity early in a child's life to communicate wonderful messages to the child. Parents have chances as long as they live to teach children a great deal about how to get and grow a self. But even parents can't do it for a child.

When I called my mother in the middle of the night to tell her that I was in labor with our first child and we were leaving for the hospital, she said, "I wish I could do this for you!" Seemed strange to me at that moment. I was excited and delighted to go and do this amazing thing. My mother knew what I didn't yet know: how large and challenging was the experience ahead. Her intention was loving and impossible. She would have deprived me of one of the most important experiences of my life. No one could do it for me, though during the long labor ahead, there were times I wished someone could and times I didn't believe I could. After eight hours of hard labor, two of them alone in a darkened birthing room pushing to crown the baby, I was given a saddle block and our baby was "delivered" by forceps.

I remember having a sense of two important parts of me. Many persons were working with the part of me that held the baby. The other part of me was all the awareness and feelings in my head and gut. No one was available for that part of me. That part of me was alone and overwhelmed. And it seemed that there was a very long distance between the two parts. Each experience with birth gave me the opportunity to coordinate these two parts. I became very accomplished at giving birth. It was never easy, and each time it pushed my limits. Giving birth was one of the things in my life that taught me I can do what I need to do. It gives me some faith about doing my dying.

That is like my experience with myself and the persons I work with in therapy. I certainly don't do it for them; I can't and I don't want to. I have my hands full with me. I have seen persons who have had unbelievable trauma in their lives do their own work to heal and grow. We can do what we need to do, even when it feels as if we can't. It just takes time and repeated opportunities to put the parts and skills together. Giving birth to a self is difficult, challenging work. It happens through the interplay between you and who you bump into. It is your work, your birthright. Don't let anyone try to take this work from you. Don't try to give it to someone else. It is impossible to give the job away, but it is not impossible to do the work. It will just feel impossible at times.

Not getting stuck in the pain

Just being alive exposes one to abandonment and abuse. What child has not had a parent's or caretaker's anger explode on her or him? Some children suffer more severe explosions. Less severity doesn't change what it is. There is no parent that can be emotionally available to a child twenty-four hours a day. We can abandon children and have no idea we have done so. Some children grow up with parents who have so little self themselves that they are hardly ever emotionally available. This can happen in vastly different situations. Typically, one might think of a very low functioning parent or a parent out of control because of chemical abuse or temper. Children are also abandoned in a very high functioning home if everything is "perfect" but no one is making room for feelings and differences. When no one is emotionally available, the child's abandonment is more subtle but just as disturbing.

We have all been hurt and disappointed in relationships,

even if, in those same relationships, we have been supported and nurtured. When hurt and disappointed, we develop our own unique coping skills to get by. We adapt. It's important to learn about those adaptations so we can make choices and decisions about how well they fit into our lives today.

In the looking and learning, we find also the times of hurt, disappointment, and anger. There is a danger here. The danger is in getting stuck in the disappointment, hurt, or anger. When we find the hard times, it is crucial to be ready to be our own healer. Taking the responsibility to be emotionally available to self at that moment changes the vulnerability that we experienced as children. Becoming frozen in the pain and focused on the offender victimizes self and allows the original pain to repeat with the same impact. The vulnerability of the child is reexperienced. When there is something that shouldn't have happened in the first place, it is tragic and devastating to reexperience the wound with the same impact. This doesn't mean that there isn't pain or anger about

> *Taking responsibility for self ends the repetition of the experience of abandonment and abuse; it means growing up from the vulnerability of childhood.*

what happened. The feelings about what happened need to be experienced and expressed. Being emotionally available to self is about being willing to help yourself, so that when you encounter an emotional memory, it doesn't communicate the same original devastating message.

For instance, people who are sexually abused as children get messages from those experiences like: "You are worthless," "You are useable," "You caused this," "You are bad." The feelings that return with flashbacks will be powerful. Persons can learn how to feel those feelings, as well as the sadness that any of the abuse ever happened in the first place, without reexperiencing those awful messages.

When today's situations replay themes and strains of yesterdays, it is very dangerous to get stuck in the hurt and anger. It is also devastating. The old messages can get reiterated in memory as well as in the present context. The stuckness, hurt, and anger can take away hope, and one's existence can become a series of reactive cycles to survive and recover from.

Taking responsibility for self

Taking responsibility for self ends the repetition of the experience of abandonment and abuse. Emotional memories will surface; present-day situations will bring those memories to life. The feelings and experience will be difficult, but there can be purpose in it. We will give ourselves new messages and change our emotional beliefs. And in the process, more self will be born.

Developing a self, an increasingly viable person, requires intention. It is not something that occurs accidentally. Growing and enhancing the inner core demands determination; it requires the constancy of focus that intention implies. In order to do that, one must decide to do that. That means recognizing and accepting that this is mine to do and it is possible for me to do it. It is not what someone deprived me of or beat out of me. Thinking that way continues to give the offender power.

It is not the work of my parents, or husband, or children. It is my work. Whether I had lots of nurturing and good support or was neglected and abused, growing up from the vulnerability of childhood means accepting the responsibility for my growth and development. If I am going to accept responsibility for the car, the checkbook, and taxes, I'm going to need myself. Maintaining responsibility for self is like dribbling in a basketball game. In order to enter the game, I have to decide to dribble the ball. There are many other essential skills and strategies involved in being able to stay in the game. I have to keep dribbling the ball while I check out what is happening on the court, while I plan and execute my strategies, and while I decide where I am going. It's possible to do, and essential if I want to play the game.

So, in order to begin, I have to decide that I will take myself on. I will be responsible for my self, and I will keep that intention and focus while I do everything else that I do.

It seems strange to have to work so hard to see that I belong to me and to talk myself into accepting responsibility for me. It is really obvious. Who else would be?! But when there are so many forces around telling me that I have value only in relation to you and that I'm responsible for your feelings, I do lose track of me. It is only a small step to assume that you must be responsible for me if I have taken on responsibility for you. Sometimes it takes the great force of life's ordeals to get one's attention to this matter. When one is quite externally focused, taking care of others and trying to prevent bad things from happening, relinquishing responsibility for self is almost complete. The anxiety that results from discovering a spouse is having an affair, for example, is exacerbated to the degree that one has been responsible for or focused on the spouse. Part of that anxiety is "What is going to happen to me?!" An important question. The anxiety and the question provoked by the ordeal can redirect one's attention back to this essential matter. One can start dribbling again, and stay in the game. The redirection of intention that the anxiety provokes allows one to get back to developing the self that is essential to have in order to be in a relationship.

Denial, distrust, and fear of feelings

Growing a self also requires the use of feelings and the development of emotional awareness. This is another area we have to be prodded back into. There is great resistance to admitting to having feelings, much less using them. Considerable time, effort, and even money are spent in the denial of feelings. The denial of feelings is frequently and importantly a survival skill, as when a child is abused. The emotional experience of the trauma gets locked out, which aids the child in surviving the trauma. Continued denial of feelings into adulthood becomes increasingly costly. One has to spend more time at working hard and dancing fast in order not to feel. Eventually anesthetics will be needed: food, cigarettes, alcohol. And then cathartics which mimic the emotional release that is needed: vomiting (bulimia), sex, anger attacks, panic attacks.

If not denied, feelings are frequently distrusted or feared. If you have been taught to hold back feelings and you do that for a long time, you may eventually explode in an outburst of anger or rage. Then, unfortunately, the learning is often "Yes, look what happens when you feel." The angry outburst serves as a reminder that feelings are to be avoided, distrusted, and feared. Anxiety can grip and shake someone who has accumulated unexpressed feelings. An anxiety attack is usually experienced as an emotional collapse, and recovery from the attack is experienced as regaining control. Consequently, the learning often is that having feelings indicates weakness and loss of control. Rage and anxiety attacks occur not because feelings have gotten out of control, but precisely because feelings have *been controlled*. Feelings need to be used. They need to be valued as the sign of aliveness and the means of empowerment—empowerment because they create awareness of what needs attention and responsible, responsive action. Power and aliveness increase when a person develops skills with feelings and learns from the experiences which the emotions create and re-create.

It seems to me that life keeps offering opportunities to learn about the value and power of feelings and emotional experiences. The experiences get larger and louder if the early opportunities aren't recognized. Not unlike debt and plastic. A new credit card carrier gets to see how the balance builds with purchases and interest and how little is whittled away by the monthly payment. Sometimes the debt has to get very large before the buyer can avoid the urge to get what he doesn't have the money for. At nuclear power plants, if early cues that something needs attention aren't heeded, the buzzers and bells get louder as the urgency for attention increases. So, I think, it is with life experiences and the importance of feelings. If we don't get it with the more quiet opportunities, life offers louder ones. I like to use my urge to prevent bad things from happening to help me hear the quieter invitations.

Getting a self

Accepting the value and power of feelings and emotional experience means accepting also that there is another way to take in and process information besides the logical, verbal, concrete intake and the linear process. The main power source is the emotional one. The verbal process can encode what resides in the emotional system, and it allows us to use the emotional information to function in the world. The emotional power source is infinite. It experiences and records everything. It holds information from those who went before us. It can receive information from that which is beyond us. No matter what we call it or how we conceptualize it, the Spirit is available through the inner core that develops by means of relationship with self. Attending to the emotional process and developing coordination between our emotional and rational systems establish the inner core that has access to where we are coming from and where we are going.

Attending to the emotional process allows awareness of needs and feelings. By knowing what one's needs and feelings are, it is possible to be in charge of and responsive to them. Learning what beliefs and meanings were made from family-of-origin experience allows that early programming to be updated and enhanced.

So getting a self is my work. I'll hook my brain back up to my gut to help in the work. I'll be bold enough to face all that is my legacy from my family of origin. I'll even ask myself to see my mom and dad as the persons they were, not as the icons of my childhood perspective. I'll see what I feel, what needs I have, and what particular skills and styles I use to cope. I'll learn how to be responsive to what I need and feel and to be responsible for how I cope. I'll use the inner core that develops and grows as I work to dig into all that I know and have experienced and to stretch through that inner core to reach all that I don't know and haven't experienced yet.

Dying to self or coming alive

The focus on self in self-work often evokes nervousness about becoming selfish. I can remember praying as a young woman to die to myself so I could live for others. My prayers were earnest and heartfelt. I was pretty successful at it. That seems like a very scary prayer now. The intention of the prayer is important. It is about being able to not be consumed with self, to reach beyond self to care about others, the world, the future. The scary part is the dying-to-myself part. That is dangerous. In dying to myself, I abandon my needs and feelings. Since my needs and feelings continue to exist after the abandonment, they will have to demand some attention without my conscious cooperation. I believe this is how I become selfish. If I don't take care of my hunger, I don't know when or how I'll try to get some of your food. If I don't take care of my need to be loved and touched, I don't know when or how I'll use your valuing of me or need to make you touch me. Selfishness is there when I am needy and desperate. If I aspire to the selflessness that is based on forgetting about me in order to serve others, my abandonment of myself and my needs will eventually have me use another person to take care of myself. At this point, selflessness and selfishness become the same—much like the point where hot and cold can feel the same.

Unlike dying to self, becoming responsible for self requires coming alive. Coming alive—not dying to self—is "the right thing to do." Alive means all systems plugged in, and I'm able to see, use, and enjoy all my senses. It means being powerful, responsive, and responsible with myself. It means having intention, being able to dribble while I walk and talk and do. Having not abandoned me, I won't be likely to use or violate you. I'll be able to experience my needs and feelings and be responsible for them. I won't act them out on you.

I need to expect responsible behavior from myself. The persons I'm in relationship with expect it from me. My husband, my children, my relatives, my office staff, my friends, my clients, even strangers I encounter expect me to behave responsibly.

My verbal expression needs to be responsible too. It is not OK to act out verbally on someone else. It frequently happens though. There are at least two ways to act out verbally. One is to rage or explode at someone. The other is to use the energy of a feeling that I'm having to talk about you. External focus allows this to happen. I've done both, especially in my parenting and in my loving with my husband. Doesn't sound very parental or loving. It wasn't, and isn't.

Expressing anger doesn't mean throwing up every feeling in my gut on the other person. It doesn't mean throwing up at all, on the other person. It also doesn't mean telling you about everything you do wrong. When I'm externally focused, throwing up and talking all about you are what I'm liable to do, and I'm likely to feel quite justified about that.

Being responsible for myself means knowing what my needs and feelings are so that I know what to do for them. Knowing what my needs and feelings are and how to take care of them becomes the basis for responsible expression. If I'm tuned into me, I can talk about me instead of you.

"I" messages have become a model for responsible verbal expression. It's tricky though. It is not possible to send a real "I" message unless I'm tuned into me. It's easy to put "I feel that…" in front of some statement about you. "I feel that you shouldn't spend money so much" definitely is not an "I" message; it's a "you" message. The "I" message would sound more like: "I feel nervous when I see you spending money; I get scared you'll run out!"

Owning your own behavior

There is a wonderful way to be able to grow in responsible behaving and expressing. It is hard though. It is being willing to look at what I have done and what I do. I call it claiming or owning my own behavior. Remember as a child hearing a teacher or parent say, "Who did this!?" and there wasn't anyone who knew anything about it? Reminds me of at least one time when I realized that something was going on with my kids. It was a spring evening just after dusk. The windows were open. I was upstairs when I heard some hushed excitement on the basketball court in the backyard. Charlie and Casey were about eight and nine years old. The whispering with their friends had some thrill to it. I strained to hear. Couldn't. As I went downstairs and entered the kitchen, Charlie was hustling out the back door, having just left the refrigerator. I called to him. No response, though I knew he had to hear me. Sure signs that something was up. I called the boys in and began an inquiry. No one knew anything. Just playing basketball and hide and seek. That would explain the flushed cheeks but not the darting eyes. I reached into the pocket of Charlie's coat, the pocket he was protecting. It was sticky and slimy in there. I pulled my hand out and there was egg shell on it. OK, now there is hard evidence; what is going on? I gave the speech about integrity and trust and admiration for the truth no matter what. Now come the excuses and the deflections. They found a bird egg and wanted to see if it was like a chicken egg. They had talked about eggs in science class. On and on went the resistance to the truth and to claiming their own behavior. We all knew the rope was getting shorter each moment. Still the resistance to owning up. Of course, the story came out eventually, or at least some of it. They had egged Mr. N's house. He had taken their ball earlier in the day when it landed in his yard.

I've come to wonder if this resistance to owning up isn't taught to kids, very carefully taught step-by-step, yet unintentionally. In our efforts to be good parents, do we believe we shouldn't be making mistakes? How many times was it obvious that we as adults had made a mistake or had done something wrong? There is relief if it doesn't come out. As the rope gets shorter, the excuses and rationalizations come in the face of increasingly obvious evidence, whether it is hard evidence like egg shells or softer evidence like flushed cheeks and nervous eyes.

I have learned the hard way that the best way to teach my kids the responsibility that I know they need is to be that responsible myself. It's humbling to own up, sometimes very painful. But it feels right and solid.

Erin's story

When she was four months old, I knew I was in trouble! My baby girl's eyes had so much vitality and energy in them. I remember the day she was lying on the bed, her eyes following me as I moved around the room. Erin was so full of life, so ready, not wanting to miss a thing. That day I remember a clear awareness: "Am I going to be up to this?!" Her spirit was so vibrant. I sensed the responsibility and challenge of being her mother. It was a mixture of excitement and anxiety. She was ready! Before she was two, she would get a determined look on her face and assert, "By YOURSELF!" She was telling me she didn't need any help. She gave love so freely, very early also. We had a ritual before bedtime. I would stand holding her next to her crib, and I would sway and sing and pray with her while she laid her head on my shoulder. At the end I would tell her how I loved her. Once she picked her head up, looked straight in my eyes, stroked each of my cheeks tenderly with her baby hands, and said, "I love you, Mommy."

Wow! Took my breath away.

At about twenty months Erin, unbeknownst to me, took her penny collection to the grocery store. At the checkout, I lost track of her for a moment. After a frantic search, I found her at the gumball machine methodically dropping each penny in and turning the crank. She had seventeen pennies. Before she was four, she pulled a step ladder from the garage and stood on it to reach the icicles hanging from the awning. When asked what she wanted for her birthday, she said, "Two packs of everything." At nine, she shaved her legs. A fantastic spirit! I loved her, enjoyed her, and was scared of her. Scared, I now realize, because I thought I had to control her. Can you imagine?! Of course it was not to be, but I tried my best, unfortunately.

It is very hard to say what I did to this child. It is hard to say because it shouldn't have happened to her. It had happened to me when I was a child; I knew how it felt. It was unthinkable to imagine I would repeat it.

When I was upset with Erin and there was some piece of behavior that needed addressing, a lesson to be taught, or a consequence to be given, I would lose control and take it far beyond that. I would start with whatever the behavior was and work up from there. Energy would pour out as I gathered more and more examples of the same behavior, then examples of related behaviors, finally a litany of everything I thought this developing little child needed to do differently. I was very critical—bad enough, but I was also sarcastic and demeaning. Tragically, the terrible things that came out of my mouth did not appall me; they were too familiar. And I was focused on disciplining my child. I know now that the energy that poured out came from every unexpressed feeling inside me. Most of the feelings were not about Erin. She was just a kid with a lot of spirit, doing kid things. The familiarity that allowed this to be so routine with me came from patterns between my mother and me.

This trance I would get into took Erin apart, as it had taken me apart years before. She would be devastated by the end, crying in her room by herself. Some of what it has left her with is that when she looks at something she needs to look at about herself, she can easily fall through the ice that I used to push her through and nearly drown in bad feelings about herself.

There were times in the middle of some of these trances that I almost got my own attention about what was happening. I could almost observe myself as I continued on. But if I had had time to go over all this in my head or with Bo before I started, I was unstoppable. I never got my own attention when I had the chance. It was Erin's pain that finally got my attention. That was familiar too, and finally I recognized it.

After a dressing down from my mom—as when she found cigarettes in my purse when I was twelve, and told me I was grounded for six weeks and she couldn't trust me to go to a coed college—my dad would comfort me. Many times I would wake in the night, after crying myself to sleep, to find my dad sitting on the edge of my bed. He would say to me, "You're a good kid." I remember him telling me once, "Your mom makes extreme statements." Oh my, isn't that the truth! She never meant to hurt me. Extreme statements come out if there are a lot of big feelings inside that you don't know what to do with.

It was Erin who provided the first intervention in this generational drama: the little nine-year-old with her hands on her hips saying, "Mother, you're projecting your feelings onto me!" I am very blessed that she came with so much spirit and courage. I began to see, and it became more difficult to repeat the trance. Still possible, however. That thing had spun out for years. It was like a 90-mile-an-hour train. It took repeated efforts to stop it and finally turn it around.

Erin's having the courage to confront me, my seeing her pain and hearing the familiar extreme statements ring in my ears—these marked the dawning of awareness. And it is awareness that broke the trance. I had to see it clearly in order to stop it. I have found that I need to speak about it too. I have had to demand of myself to say out loud, "It's happening right now." Or to go back and say, "I just did some of it again." I have to say it out loud; that is what stops me. I have had great desire to get this stopped.

Speaking aloud

There are other times when I *have to* speak about it. As I've worked on myself and felt my own stuff, I have gone to my children and husband and asked them to hear what I had learned. During and after my dad's death came many realizations about my experience in my family of origin, and with them came realizations about my actions with our family. I had to go tell my children and husband what I realized and take responsibility for my actions with them. These were powerful, precious moments between us. They would draw close and listen and reach out to me at the most painful disclosures. I felt so clear then, and the differences between us were so clear that we could stand very close to each other.

I'll tell another story about the other times when I have had to speak about what I've done. This story is about Erin again, though similar stories could be told involving each of the other children or my husband. One morning about two years ago, I found Erin in bed crying. She had been crying a lot. Her eyes were swollen; she had already used ice to try to soothe them. She was dismayed as to why she was crying so hard. I asked what had happened as I sat next to her on the bed. She told me the story of how a friend who was angry with her had gotten in her car at the end of the previous evening and begun telling Erin why she was angry. The friend told Erin two things that she was angry about; then she told her ways she saw her do similar things with other people. Soon she was telling Erin all that was wrong with her and everything she should change. Through her tears, Erin told me she knew that her friend was not right about all of this and that it was her friend's anger that had escalated the situation. She realized this, but still she cried. As I listened and looked at her, I knew why her reaction to her friend was so large. I said, "Erin, don't you see?" Her swollen eyes widened: "What?" This was not all about her encounter with her friend. "This is what I did when I would get upset with you. I would start and build and attack, and you were just a little girl then." We held each other; Erin cried, but more calmly now. It was another powerful and precious time. Each of us was so clear and separate that we felt deep closeness. I felt the truth of what I had said deep inside me. It felt solid and freeing.

154

"How do I do this?"

This is one of the most important things I've learned to do with my awareness of my experience in my family of origin: to see that I carry on the painful patterns and to see when and how I do it. I then ask myself to be willing to claim it out loud. When I realize something difficult that I experienced as a child, I help myself with it and give myself a new message about it. Then I ask, "And how do I do this?" When I see some behavior in a person that I don't like, I try to interrupt the judgment or criticism I might make by asking "How do I do this?" Sometimes it's tricky because I may do it in a way that, to me at least, seems not the same, not so flagrant. But when I look, I find how I do it. Then, at least, I can make a decision to do it or not. I can choose to be more how I want to be by learning how I am and seeing what I want to do about it.

I remember once watching a woman be very critical of her husband. She interrupted her conversation to make a comment about and an adjustment to what he was saying in another conversation. I wanted to relish my indignance that someone could presume to be so right! Inside me, I recognized the same critical/controlling pattern from my family of origin, and so I asked the question, "How do I do this?" No answer. Later that evening with the question still in my head, I found myself lifting the lid on the chili my husband had made for supper and asking him if he had been sure to put this and that in. He was polite and firm.

This was his chili and his kitchen for the night, he told me, and would I like to go read the paper, please? Nice. He wouldn't let me get away with it. And I had my answer: "That's one way I do it!"

"Are you laughing at me?"

It has been very important for me to learn that criticism and ridicule are parts of my family pattern. I needed to learn how decimated I can feel by criticism and ridicule, so that I can help myself when that happens. Especially to learn to stand by so that my whole self doesn't fall in a hole. It's helpful to know that is why I'm sometimes uncomfortable when there is laughter about something I've done. There's a part of me whose eyes get big and she wonders, "Are you laughing at me?!" Uncovering all this has set me free to laugh at myself and enjoy my own folly. What a relief! Those awarenesses are very important. They open me up and allow me to grow. That's wonderful.

That growth, freedom, and openness feel right for me to enjoy and thrive in if I am vigilant about not passing the destructive stuff on. It feels solid and trustworthy every time I own what I do or have done. I need to keep doing that. I don't expect to get over having to do that.

The legacy of family

The family patterns of worrying, criticism, and ridicule that I have referred to are part of the dysfunction of my family of origin. Of course, there is more. And, of course, our generational accumulation is packed with splendid, solid patterns and traditions.

The family I came from knows how to celebrate. My mother could bring a glow to holidays and special events. When I was little, she and I used to pretend "Mrs. Brown and Mrs. Smith" in the kitchen while she ironed. My mother was a storyteller; she could bring times of long ago to life in a way that was enthralling. We prayed together at meals and at night, and we knelt with each other in the living room of our home before every trip we took. My mom baked and cooked for families in the neighborhood when there was illness. She was not afraid to stand very near when there was dying. My mother was gracious and kind. Her family had some wonderful craziness in it. Their communication carried affection in their humor with each other. The humor could get nonsensical and outrageous. There was an extravagance in the air that extended to generosity, welcoming, and magic moments.

My dad's family brought a parade of warm, capable women and tender, competent men. I saw women who were intelligent and astute, women whose interests were many and not superficial. They were erect, wide-eyed women with a calm and loving presence. My uncles and cousins have been spiritual men— ministry and artistry among their pursuits. I watched and listened as these men spoke with care and concern about life's issues and explored history and solutions. There was always time for people in this family. Affection was shown with calm, steadfast touching and support. My father was an exceptionally bright man, who worked very hard and who enjoyed very simple pleasures. He was generous to a fault. My dad's eyes lit up with pride, love, and joy at the sight of any of his children or grandchildren. My dad could be conned into breaking a rule if it wasn't too important, and he was ethical and honest down to his bones.

I have been blessed in the legacy of my family. There is so much to cherish. And there has been some powerful stuff to change. One doesn't make the other go away. Our kids have the legacies we have both brought, the one our joining created, our continued efforts at change and growth, and the changes their growing has demanded of our family. There is much for them to cherish and also some powerful stuff for them to change.

Family patterns that get carried on through the years are like a message passed from person to person. The message does not resemble itself at the end. Generational patterns originate for one reason and get perpetuated for many different ones. Taking responsibility to see not only how we were affected by these patterns but also how we participate in passing them on has an awesome effect. Destructive generational patterns can be broken, and the spirit of the family can be enhanced and expanded.

The interests of everyone are served. Becoming responsible for ourselves teaches responsibility to our children. The family becomes more capable and gets to thrive in its unique ways freer from dysfunction.

Taking responsibility: implications for society

If families can learn and grow in this way, can societies? I know that parents and teachers can't get anywhere with kids on alcohol and drug use without becoming responsible with their own decisions about substances. And it doesn't work to hit a kid and admonish, "Don't hit your brother!" Countless times I have seen parents take responsibility for their own behavior in family sessions. What happens next is respect, distinction, and empowerment. As the parents' actions follow up on the statement of responsibility, young people take off in their own growth and development.

Taking responsibility is not about self-blame or self-shame. It

Coming alive means allowing feelings, learning from them, and getting skillful with them. It means letting the responsiveness that develops empower you to be responsible and to enjoy and celebrate.

is about becoming powerful. Taking responsibility is an ability that relies on and develops out of internal relatedness. It is an ability that develops out of being powerful enough to recognize shameful behavior and powerful enough to claim it without collapsing in shame and guilt. Denial is designed to protect against just such a collapse of self-esteem. The internal relatedness, that deep sense of our own life and spirit and value, holds us up right alongside the behavior that needs owning up to. The things we have done, our own dysfunction and destructiveness, are not all that we are. They need not take us apart. The fullness and goodness of who we are need not be demolished by the shameful things we have done. We need our fullness and goodness to do something about our shameful acts.

As a society, we are full of wonder, promise, and brightness. We have also tragedy, hypocrisy, and prejudice entangling our spirit as a nation. One does not make the other go away. We need not deny or hang our heads in shame at the shameful patterns that threaten to strangle us. We need to get our heads up and look straight in the eye of the destructive patterns in the society of our origin and find out how we are involved in passing those patterns on. Our brightness and promise will be support and resource in the process.

We want abusing moms and dads to stop and come back to life to give their dear babies the care and safety they deserve. I cannot ask an abusing mom or dad to do that if I am not in-

volved in the same pursuit of becoming more alive and responsible. If I am, I'll have credibility with them, and we can learn
and grow alongside each other.

Blaming, better-than-you stances, and disgust won't raise
anybody up. Those things elevate some of us by having some
stand on top of others. Then we need to be sure to keep others
down so we can feel better about ourselves. Denial of feelings,
of the past, of dysfunction in our families, of our unsavory actions keeps us running away from ourselves and trampling on
others so we can stand higher.

Coming alive

There is no perfection. We don't have to look so "good" or
feel so "fine." We just have to learn to walk and chew gum at
the same time and learn to come alive. Walking and chewing
gum means learning how to keep track of the stuff we need to
work on while basking in our accomplishments, and how to
hold onto our value and goodness while in full awareness of our
mistakes and offenses. Walking and chewing gum can also
mean that, when I have a feeling, your feeling doesn't have to
go away. And if you are different from me, neither of us has to
change. And if families have trouble and dysfunction, that
doesn't wipe out their wonderful stuff.

Coming alive means allowing feelings, learning from them,
and getting skillful with them. Coming alive means letting the

responsiveness that develops empower you to be responsible and to enjoy and celebrate. The responsiveness and aliveness within will flow out to others according to the uniqueness of all that you are and came from.

Your own story can raise you up, fill you with your spirit, and enrich all your relationships. Being able to feel and to learn from all that went before makes life a powerful, joyful journey to all that comes after.